1000 Years
of Irish
Whiskey

FIRST PUBLISHED 1980 BY THE O'BRIEN PRESS
11 CLARE STREET DUBLIN 2 IRELAND

©

COPYRIGHT RESERVED
ISBN 0 - 905140 - 71 - 0

JACKET DESIGN: MICHAEL O'BRIEN/DEBBY BELL
BOOK DESIGN: MICHAEL O'BRIEN
TYPESETTING: DESIGN & ART FACILITIES, DUBLIN
BINDING: JOHN F. NEWMAN
PRINTED IN THE REPUBLIC OF IRELAND
BY IRISH ELSEVIER PRINTERS

"1000 Years
of Irish
Whiskey"

Malachy Magee

O'BRIEN
PRESS

Contents

Left —
A lost art, a cooper at work at
Jameson's Distillery Dublin.

Preface

Irish whiskey is today reaching out across the world, making new friends and admirers in many lands. It is a worthy ambassador for Ireland, a fine quality product that is welcomed and appreciated everywhere.

Uisce beatha has a long and eventful history behind it. In endeavouring to put together in popular form some of the more remarkable and interesting episodes recorded along the way I have searched out a wide range of available sources of information. I have also sought advice on technical and other aspects from knowledgeable and ever helpful authorities, to all of whom I express my indebtedness.

This account is not intended to be a definitive history of the subject. Part of the colourful story of Irish whiskey is entangled in the roots of folklore, which possibly adds a touch of the fanciful to the factual here and there.

Irish whiskey is a product of the same soil that gives us our staple foods. It is a gift of Nature, an elixir that can be beneficial in many ways – provided it is used in moderation and with the respect it deserves. Indeed to abuse this great spirit by over-indulgence can be a regrettable exercise in self-punishment.

'A sovereign drink, the chroniclers declare, if it be taken orderlie – beware of surfeit.'

Malachy Magee

Chapter 1

Celtic Magic

 THE IRISH believe they make the finest whiskey in the world. The Scots put forth a similar claim. What is indisputable is that both these ancient Celtic nations have, for centuries, possessed the art, the skills and the means to produce, each in its own way, *uisce beatha* of peerless quality.

It's a gladsome feeling just to raise your glass of Irish and observe its elusive glint of gold, to inhale its distinctively subtle aroma, or 'nose' and, finally, to savour the taste that delights the palate and warms the spirit. It's interesting also to reflect that your glass of Irish took perhaps ten years to produce, and has behind it a thousand years of tradition.

Nobody can say for sure how or when it all began, but it is almost certain that whiskey, *uisce beatha*, or water of life, was first produced in Ireland. It is reckoned that the art of distillation was brought by Irish missionaries from the Mediterranean regions about 500 or 600 A.D. It would appear that distilling, like most of the early sciences, came from the East. Its first European practice was in Spain, introduced by the Moors in the Middle Ages. Perfumes and aromatics were being distilled long before potable spirits.

The word 'whiskey' is believed to have been coined by the soldiers of King Henry II who invaded Ireland in the 12th century and discovered the delights of the native *uisce beatha*. The old Gaelic name bothered them, however, and their crude anglicisation subsequently became assimilated into common speech.

The much-travelled Irish monks, it is also thought, carried the secrets of *uisce beatha* to the isles and highlands of Scotland. And it was the Scots who proceeded eventually to capitalise on the bountiful gift of nature by sending it to grateful lands around the world.

Irish whiskey is made today in much the same manner as it has been all down the centuries, and with the same basic ingredients—the best of Irish barley and other cereals, and pure clear water. To these must be added the benefits of the sparkling Irish climate which makes it all possible, and time itself—lots and lots of time.

The story of Irish whiskey is both turbulent and dramatic. There are tales of passion and violence, of corruption and skullduggery, of political intrigue and commercial duplicity. And there are the wily poitín men, whose sharp wits and instinct for survival generally kept them a jump or two ahead of the excise men, their natural enemy. Battles were fought and blood was spilled between the men who made and smuggled the illegal spirit and the men whose duty it was to suppress it. And of course there was humour also in the lusty adventures of those lawless days.

Irish whiskey became the focus of historic court proceedings, where controversial judgements on the relative merits of 'Irish' and 'Scotch' led to the establishment of royal commissions of inquiry. Political power behind the native Irish whiskey industry forced the Chancellor of the Exchequer to abandon his plan to impose punitive taxation on the sale of the spirit. Because Irish distillers refused to compromise on the traditional quality of their product they had to sacrifice their predominant hold on the important English market.

The one revolutionary change in the manufacturing process began about 1830, with the introduction of the Coffey still, also known as the continuous or patent still. This invention was to send shock waves through the conservative Irish distilling industry, and indeed the tremors continued right up until fairly recent times. The new apparatus produced an almost flavourless spirit which, when blended with the older pot still whiskey, created a lighter milder beverage.

The patent still process showed itself to be faster and more economical than the cumbersome pot still method, which in Ireland involved three distinct distillations, as against two preferred by the malt distillers of the Scottish highlands. This additional distillation gave the Irish whiskey a somewhat lighter taste than the traditional Scotch malts. The new invention found no favour with the Irish pot still men, who contended that its produce was a spurious concoction, and certainly not whiskey.

In its early years the Coffey still was used mainly for the production of industrial spirit and also in the manufacture of gin. It was not until the 1850s that Andrew Usher of Edinburgh, a prominent wine and spirit dealer, began to experiment in combining the new spirit with pot still whiskey. Thus was born Scotland's blended whiskey industry. Its produce was known as grain whiskey, as distinct from malt, and the man who made it all possible, the inventor of the patent still on which the Scotch whisky fortunes were founded, was an Irishman, Aeneas Coffey, one-time Inspector-General of British Excise in Ireland.

A traditional way of storing whiskey.

Chapter 2

Old Tradition and New Technology

IN THEORY, whiskey-making is a simple process, as any poitín man could tell you. All he needs for his trade is a mash of grain, some yeast, a bowl, a kettle, a jar for the distillation and a receptacle for condensing the vapour.

Basically, the traditional pot still methods have not changed. But if the old moonshiners of long ago could today walk around the modern distilling complex at Midleton, Co. Cork, they would be dazzled by the array of equipment on view, symbolising the combination of engineering skill and scientific knowledge which generate today's great export industry.

And yet, notwithstanding the technological advances, the traditional personal touch is still required in order to produce the famous Irish pot still whiskey. The entire distilling process must still be directed with instinctive skill and judgment by the distiller and his still-men, a proficiency which comes only with years of experience. And the distillery men continue to use the ancient terms which baffle the layman, strange words like grists, worts, worms, washes, tuns, kieves and backs. The huge still is the kettle, complete with spout.

Irish whiskey is made from a mixture of malted and unmalted barley, with the addition of yeast, for fermenting purposes, and water. Malting the barley is a separate process. It is, in effect, the germination of the grain, allowing the starches in the barley to be converted into fermentable sugar. In the traditional method, the barley is screened and graded, and left steeping in water for two or three days. The sodden barley is then spread out in the malthouse floor where germination begins with a 'sweating' process. The malting barley is watched and turned regularly by men with wooden shovels, or *shiels,* over a period of about eight days.

The maltster has to determine exactly when to halt the germination process. This is done by drying off the malting barley in the coal-fired kilns for a couple of days. The new malt is then bagged and stored until required by the distiller. The screenings, known as malt combings, are sold for animal feed. This was the time-honoured method followed until quite recently. Today the process is effected by more sophisticated means, and huge revolving drums are used in the malting operation.

The malt mix contains a substance called diastase, which turns the starch in the unmalted grain into sugar, which is later converted into alcohol by the action of yeast. Any starch-rich cereal can be used in making whiskey, but Irish distillers have always preferred barley which, when mixed with malt, gives Irish whiskey its subtly distinctive flavour, coming somewhere between the light Scotch grain whisky and the Highland malts.

The barley mix is ground into a fine meal in preparation for the brewing stage. It is then conveyed into the distillery's large mash tuns, or kieves. Hot water is pumped in, and the mash is rhythmically stirred and beaten up by a system of mechanical rakes. The wort, as the mash is now called, is cooled off and pumped into receivers known as fermenting backs, great circular vessels which hold about 30,000 gallons. The yeast is now introduced, and this sets up a bubbly agitation in the sluggish wort, which builds up gradually into a raging ferment. Slowly the storm subsides and alcohol is made. The wort has now become the wash, ready for the final and intricate distilling stage.

Distilling simply means heating a liquid until it turns into a vapour and then condensing the vapour back into liquid. Alcohol boils at a lower temperature than water and it is the function of the still to trap the vapour from the fermented mixture and condense it into spirit. Whiskey distillate retains the flavour of the original grain.

The wash is pumped into the wash still, a huge copper kettle of perhaps 70,000 gallons capacity, formerly heated by a glowing furnace but nowadays by steam. When the wash comes to the boil the vapours are conveyed along the lyne arm or 'spout' of the kettle into the worm, a long coil of copper tubing immersed in cold

An old photograph showing a view of the Old Bushmills Distillery
in Co. Antrim.

The new Midleton Distillery, showing from left, the still house,
yeast propagation, brewhouse, grain tower and by-products recovery.

water. The worm condenses the alcohol vapours into spirit which passes into a receiving vat.

This first-run spirit is called low wines and is considered too heavy and oily to make whiskey, so it is returned for a further distillation. The second distillate is known as feints, and this may contain unwanted substances also. A third distillation is needed to extract a spirit which contains only the minimum amount of volatile flavours and essential oils, a spirit that will eventually mature into whiskey.

Even this thrice-distilled spirit is carefully scrutinised and controlled in the search for perfection. This calls for the skill and judgement of the distiller. The spirit is run through the spirit safe, a glass-sided box, and the stillman, using his experienced eye and intuition, as well as his special instruments, keeps testing the spirit until he is fully satisfied about the quality. In general, only the middle part of the run meets his exacting requirements. The foreshot, or first of the run, can be too strong and heavy, and the end of the run, the feints, tends to be weak.

When the stillman is satisfied, by sight and test, of the required strength and quality he switches the run to the receiving vat. The foreshots and feints are diverted back for a future distillation.

Young whiskey is harsh, colourless and unpalatable. Its strength is about 50° overproof and must be reduced to the required maturation strength by the addition of pure water. The spirit is filled into oak casks and transported to the warehouses, or bonded stores, under the watchful eyes of the excise officers who, indeed, have been present throughout the entire distilling process. In the great cloister-like vaults the whiskey begins its long silent sleep for five to fifteen years. In the former Jameson distillery in Bow Street, extending wide and deep under the heart of Dublin, about two million gallons of maturing whiskey were stored at any one time.

In the cool darkness nature works her slow miracle which no man understands completely. The oak casks, which allow the spirit to 'breathe', a cool even temperature, and the long sleep all contribute to the mysterious alchemy which gradually changes an untamed fiery spirit into an impeccably mellow whiskey.

14

Chapter 3

The Coffey Revolution

 COMPARATIVELY little is known about the personal background of Aeneas Coffey, the man whose invention radically changed the entire spirits industry. He was born in Dublin about 1780, educated at Trinity College, and entered the Excise service around 1800 as a gauger, and eventually became Inspector General of Excise in Ireland. British Customs & Excise records show that he was appointed Sub-Commissioner of Inland Excise and Taxes for the district of Drogheda in 1813, and that he finally resigned from the service at his own request in 1824. He was clearly a zealous and dedicated law enforcer, feared by the nomadic manufacturers of illicit whiskey. He was also involved in violent clashes with the smugglers.

Coffey was a man of exceptional engineering and inventive skills. His patent still, which carries his name, was the instrument on which the great Scotch blended whiskey industry was founded. It was no fault of Coffey's that it also brought about a serious decline in the fortunes of Irish whiskey.

On his retirement from service Coffey went into the distilling business and for a short time ran the Dock Distillery in Grand Canal Street, Dublin.

In a paper published by the *Dublin Historical Record* in February, 1947, entitled "Aeneas Coffey and his Patent Still," historian J. J. Kerr recalls that he was unable to trace any record of Coffey's death or burial. He was married and had one son, Aeneas junior, who worked for a time with his father in the business in their premises at Barrow Street, Dublin, but later went to South Africa to manage a patent still distillery. He married in that country but his wife died and there were no children. Aeneas junior subsequently returned to England and

John Jameson & Sons' Distillery at Bow Street Dublin, 1878.

lived in Kingston, Surrey.

Coffey probably had in mind a system for the production of a pure spirit for industrial purposes. In making whiskey the spirit must retain the flavouring elements of its original materials, notably the malted barley, as well as the traces of volatile substances known collectively as fusel oils, which help to give pot still whiskey its eventual distinctive character and 'nose'. The patent still process eliminates all but the most minute traces of these elements, producing neutral spirit which is used for blending purposes.

Coffey was not the first in the field with the new type still. Several versions were introduced in the quest of perfecting a method of producing pure spirit in a continuous stream, but it was the Irishman who made the breakthrough with his improved design. Indeed the original Coffey still remains basically unchanged today, although, of course, progressive improvements have evolved.

Coffey installed his new still in his Dublin distillery and later set up a business to manufacture the continuous still. He offered it first to the numerous Irish distilleries of the time, but all except one or two small concerns rejected the new apparatus. With traditional conservatism Irish distillers argued that genuine whiskey could only be made by the time-honoured pot still method.

Coffey then turned to the Scottish distilleries, which at that time largely manufactured all-malt whiskies. He had more success there. Quite a few distilleries installed his still in order to sell its produce for industrial purposes. Other potentially lucrative markets were the "gin mills" of London. The strong neutral spirit produced by the Coffey still was especially suitable for making gin, then the biggest selling drink in England.

The Coffey patent still is a more compact, and certainly much more complex apparatus than the conventional "kettles" of the pot still system. It comprises twin columns, 40 to 50 feet high, each divided into a series of compartments separated by perforated metal plates. The first column, called the analyser, separates the spirit from the wash, and the second column, the rectifier, further concentrates the spirit by removing unwanted fusel oils.

Steam from the boiler is admitted into the base of the

analyser and pumped upwards, the wash is piped to the top of the rectifier from which it circulates through each compartment by means of an elaborate winding piping system, being heated in the process. It is then carried to the top of the analyser and allowed to travel down the column through each perforated plate. The alcohol becomes vaporised as it meets the upcoming steam, which forces the spiritous vapours out through the top of the analyser, and these are piped into the base of the rectifier. Passing up through the perforated plates the vapours are gradually stripped of their fusel oils, and on reaching the spirit plate near the top of the column have become concentrated spirit which is then drawn off into a cooling condenser.

Continuous still spirit is 60 degrees overproof or more, as against an approximate 50 degrees in the case of pot still. As the flavour of the grain is practically eliminated in the distilling, cereals like maize and rye are used extensively in the continous still, as well as barley. As with the pot still process there are foreshots and tails which are returned to the wash for further distilling. Grain whiskey, as the patent still produce is called, is casked for maturation in the warehouses for the compulsory three-year period, but unlike pot whiskey it does not improve significantly.

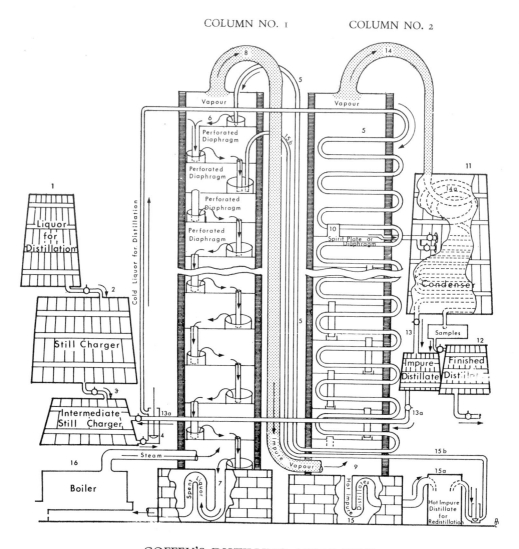

COLUMN NO. 1   COLUMN NO. 2

COFFEY'S DISTILLING APPARATUS

Order of process—1. Vat for crude liquor. 2. Charger for Still. 3. Additional Charger. 4. Pump. 5. Pipe conveying liquor to be distilled. Col. No. 2 containing No. 5 Pipe, impure Vapour from Col. 1 and spirit plate where hot distillate is drawn off. Col. No. 1 containing liquor descending from diaphragm to diaphragm and ascending steam from boiler. 6. Liquor spreading over diaphragm. 7. Spent liquor. 8. Vapour from steam and liquor to bottom of Col. 2. 9. Vapour ascending to Col. 2. 10. Plate where hot product condensed is drawn off. 11. Hot product condenser. 12. Finished product 13. Impure product for re-distillation. 13[a]. Impure product to Still charger. 14. Uncondensed vapour to be condensed in 14[a] and conveyed by 13 and 13[a] to Still Charger 15. Impure spirit liquid for re-distillation through 15[a] and 15[b] to Col. No. 1. 16. Steam boiler. Drawing adapted from *Evidence before the Royal Commission on Whiskey and Other Potable Spirits, 1908*.

Chapter 4

Pot Still or Blended?

THE FOUR MAIN Dublin distilleries operating around the middle of the 19th century sold their pot still whiskey in bulk to dealers and publicans. They were justifiably suspicious that some of these customers were less scrupulous than others and engaged themselves in the more profitable and more nefarious practice of mixing some inferior liquor with the first quality Dublin whiskey.

The big four distillers of the time were John Jameson & Son of Bow Street, William Jameson & Co. of Marrowbone Lane, John Power & Son of John's Lane, and George Roe & Co. of Thomas Street. They had the highest standards; they produced the finest whiskey in the world and had an unchallenged home and export trade. They ran their businesses on strictly conservative lines, using the best equipment and were good employers. There were a dozen or more smaller distilleries around the country, all of them regarded, it would seem, with a certain disdain by the metropolitan manufacturers as being of an inferior class.

There were four distilleries in Cork city and another one in nearby Midleton, the largest in the area. These five companies came together in 1867 to form the Cork Distilleries Company Limited and offer stern competition to the Dublin companies. Another of the provincial distilleries of the time was Daly's of Tullamore, founded in 1829, which was to outlast two of Dublin's big four.

The Jamesons, the Powers and the Roes were quite properly aggrieved at the thought of their admirable products being subjected to malpractice in trading and being 'adulterated' by the addition of what they disparagingly referred to as 'coarse provincial whiskey.'

They had little legal redress at the time to put a stop to these transgressions unless they could produce incontrovertible evidence, even though some traders brazenly pushed the whiskey mixture into the smaller taverns under their own names.

But these dishonest dealings were comparatively trivial in the face of a sinister new development that was building up in the whiskey trade and causing increasing alarm in the stately boardrooms of the Dublin distilleries.

During the 19th century these firms enjoyed a lucrative export trade with England and its colonies, including India, Australia, Canada as well as America. In England Irish pot still practically monopolised the whiskey market. The Scotch malts came from numerous small Highland distilleries and each had its own flavoursome peculiarities, satisfying local tastes. But to the English consumer no two Scotch whiskies tasted alike. In general terms the Scotch malts had a heavy, peaty taste, a distinction that was demanded in Scotland but which found little favour with the less rugged English drinkers. Irish was preferred because its malted and unmalted barley mixture gave a lighter whiskey of consistent quality and flavour.

During the 1860s many Coffey stills appeared in Scotland and Northern Ireland, and one or two in the South. 'Blended whiskey' was beginning to make its way into the market. It was manufactured and sold considerably cheaper than pot still. But in most cases the 'blended whiskey' tag was dubious to say the least, consisting of patent still spirit and given some substance and flavour by the addition of small amounts of pot still whiskey. Scotland was still a long way off from the development of the great branded blends of later years, and the various concoctions hastily pushed into the growing market led to acrimonious disputes in the trade.

The big four Dublin distilleries, serene in the knowledge that their long-established and aged in the wood whiskey was beyond reproach, were for the first time jolted out of their complacency. They saw their hitherto unchallenged trading supremacy on the English market being breached and buffeted. Dublin pot still whiskey was being pushed aside and left unsold as an undiscerning public turned to a cheaper and spurious beverage, a kind of 'instant whiskey.'

22

The still house in Jameson's Bow Street Distillery, now disused.

The Irish companies consoled themselves with the belief that customers would soon come to the realisation that this new patent still spirit mixture was in no way comparable with Irish pot whiskey and would eventually be rejected in favour of the old traditional drink.

Fortunately for the Irish distillers their home market customers shared their views and regarded the new whiskey as an inferior substitute for the real thing. But what added anger to injury as far as the distillers were concerned, and caused them much more alarm than the decline in profits, was that the new spirit was being marketed as Irish whiskey. Many of the Scottish patent still operators and dealers, shrewdly aware of the Englishman's traditional preference for Irish whiskey, bought up quantities of Irish for the mixing procedure.

In their boardrooms the Dublin directors considered ways and means of countering the new threat. One suggestion was that they enter the patent still business themselves in direct challenge to the Scottish and some Ulster manufacturers. But this proposal was coldly received and quickly dismissed. The Dublin and leading provincial distillery directors were practically unanimous in the view that the new product was not true whiskey.

They decided to join forces and launch a campaign to publicise the facts of the situation and expose these 'fraudulent practices' in the industry.

Thus began, in the 1870s, the great whiskey controversy, which was to rumble on for more than half a century, resounding periodically through Press and Parliament, a recurring headache for successive British Chancellors, with bitter allegations and arguments, stern debates in Westminster, select committees reporting back and forth; eventually it resulted in a royal commission of inquiry and forced reluctant changes in Government budgetary plans.

It also brought about radical changes in the distilling industry, which saw Scotch blended whiskey, after early years of free-for-all scrambling, eventually attaining quality standards which, backed by skilful business acumen, won for it international repute and an export trade of paramount importance to the British economy.

Chapter 5

The Whiskey War

THE PATENT STILL business was given a significant boost in 1860 when the revenue authorities agreed to allow blending of 'plain British spirit' in bond, and dealers were permitted to bring the spirit from any part of the United Kingdom to any other part and mix it with any other spirit of British manufacture in any proportions.

This concession came as a further setback to the Irish distillers. Pot still whiskey from Ireland and Scotland was traditionally left to mature and mellow in casks for years, although this was not compulsory. Patent still spirit was not generally subjected to this costly treatment, although the more reputable firms did in fact put the spirit down in bonded warehouses for lengthy periods. And so in the 1860-70s the patent still spirit, flavoured with a dash of Irish or Scotch pot still, was poured on the market almost straight from the Coffey still.

Cargoes of the spirit were carried regularly from Glasgow and Liverpool to Dublin and Belfast, to be compounded with perhaps ten to twenty per cent of the pot still distillation and promptly shipped back to England to be marketed as Dublin or Irish whiskey. The lighter taste, and the cheaper price, evidently appealed to London drinkers, even wooing many of them away from gin, which had long since supplanted rum as the most favoured spirit beverage. As the sales of the new whiskey drink rose steadily Irish pot still gradually yielded its hold on the market, preferred only by the more discriminating and more affluent drinkers.

The whiskey boom was given a further push about this time by the virtual disappearance from the market of Cognac brandy, brought about by the phylloxera disease

The Port of Dublin at the turn of the last century.

which ravaged the Cognac vineyards and caused enormous economic damage. This disease is transmitted by tiny insects which attack the roots of the vine. In the 1880s much of the Cognac area was threatened with extinction by the scourge which caused a complete breakdown in the production of brandy, and the effects of which were felt for the next fifty years.

New distilleries were built in Scotland and new whiskey dealing firms appeared. Several smaller distilleries in Ireland, notably in the North, joined the bandwagon and Coffey stills were set up, in many cases side by side with pot stills, in Belfast, Derry, Dundalk, Cork and Limerick, practically all of whose grain spirit output was exported. Much of the blending, or mixing, was done by the dealers, who bought from distilleries and sold directly to the pubs.

Competition for a share of the market became so intense that, inevitably, a price war developed and some less scrupulous firms resorted to dubious cost-cutting and used inferior mixtures. One such notorious beverage of the period was a cheap German importation known as 'Hamburg' Sherry and used by some dealers as the flavouring essence for the spirit.

The Dublin distillers were stung into action. They commissioned and published a series of pamphlets in the early 1870s, later published in book form under the title of *Truths About Whiskey*. They accused entrepreneurs in the industry of engaging in illicit trading practices with the 'silent spirit' as they disdainfully called the Coffey still produce, silent because it had no distinctive qualities and told no tales of its origin. They were given significant moral support from an unlikely quarter when a leading article in the prestigious *London Times* of February 1st, 1876, roundly condemned 'the fraudulent imitations masquerading as Irish whiskey.' Similar sentiments were expressed by the *Daily Telegraph* which also devoted considerable editorial space to the matter.

Indeed the subject of the new taste in whiskey was for many years a recurring and controversial topic in the editorial and correspondence columns of newspapers and journals. Accusations of high profit and low quality were thrown at the unheeding heads of some producers. Even that austere medical journal, *The Lancet*, felt constrained to enter the fray from time to time with stern warnings

A busy dockside scene at Dublin's Custom House.

about the dangers of consuming premature spirit of dubious origin.

A contemporary of *The Lancet,* the *Medical Examiner,* also deemed it necessary to alert its practitioner readers to exercise extreme care in prescribing small amounts of whiskey in appropriate instances, and to distinguish the genuine from the spurious. It outlined briefly the manufacturing processes of first quality whiskey, using only the finest barley malt and selected cereals, the distilling system and the slow years of maturation in deep cellars. It continued: '...The manufacturing of Irish whiskey was almost monopolised a few years ago by four great distilling firms in Dublin, but the products of these firms were supplied to the public by the intervention of middlemen who had no stills and had never made a drop of whiskey, but who issued advertisements and placards and who thus became known as the whiskey people, and kept the actual makers in the background.

'In process of time these middlemen saw their way to make larger profits by diluting new, or coarse genuine whiskey with rectified spirit, and more recently, emboldened by success, they have sold vast quantities of spirit which contains no whiskey at all, but is simply a medicinal tincture, composed of rectified spirit, and of various flavouring substances known only to themselves. The rectified spirit is made by what is called a patent still which brings over only ethylic alcohol and water from the fermented liquor supplied to it, and this fermented liquor may be made from damaged grain, rotten potatoes, refuse molasses or any other waste which contains a sufficiency of glucose or starch.

'The rectified spirit thus produced is called silent spirit because it brings over no flavour. Being made from refuse it is much cheaper than whiskey, and it is chemically pure, or nearly so. When made into a tincture it is ready for immediate consumption and it is then sold under the name of whiskey, often with some grand distinctive title and at a low price.'

In furtherance of their cause the Irish distillers were not slow to enlist the aid of influential friends in Parliament. One of their ablest spokesmen at Westminster was the member for Limerick, William O'Sullivan, who just happened to be in the wine and spirit business himself.

O'Sullivan was an ardent and eloquent advocate in the cause of the Irish whiskey industry and in a series of speeches, amendments and debates, from 1874-77, he left the Government, the House of Commons and public opinion in no doubt as to the abuses it was being subjected to. His reforming campaign achieved little in the way of legislative action but he built up considerable sympathy and support, much of which was translated into continuing pressure on the Government for the next twenty-five years. It was not until 1890 that they conceded, in the face of public opinion, to demands for an investigation into aspects of the blended whiskey trade by agreeing to the appointment of a Parliamentary Select Committee of Inquiry.

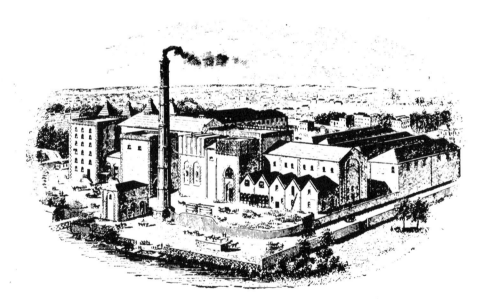

Jones's Road Distillery, Dublin.

Chapter 6

Press and Parliament

ON APRIL 10th, 1875, William O'Sullivan rose in the House of Commons to move an amendment to the Adulteration of Food and Drugs Bill, then in committee, the object of which, he said, was to prevent the sale of a compound known as silent whiskey. He drew the attention of the House 'to the system which prevails in Her Majesty's bonding stores in Ireland of allowing a cheap spirit imported from Scotland to be mixed in these stores with Irish whiskey and reshipped direct from there to this country under bond, which leads the purchaser to believe he is buying Irish whiskey, a fraudulent practice calculated to injure the high character which Irish whiskey enjoys in the markets of the world.'

Mr. O'Sullivan was persuaded to withdraw his amendment after the Chancellor, Sir Stafford Northcote, assured him he would be afforded a private conference with the Chancellor and officers of the Customs and Excise to discuss any grievances he might have in this matter.

It would appear that nothing emerged from this under-taking and a year later O'Sullivan was demanding that a Select Committee of the House be appointed 'to inquire into the practice, sanctioned by the Government, of blending, and thereby adulterating, Irish whiskey in Her Majesty's Customs stores in Ireland.'

He pointed out that the patent still grain spirit could be purchased for 2s 8d a gallon while Irish pot still whiskey cost 6s a gallon, and large quantities of 'this adulterated spirit lay in Government stores and went out as Irish whiskey and under the same permit as genuine Irish whiskey, thus deceiving the buyer and his customer.'

He quoted some figures from investigations he had made to emphasise his arguments. At the Custom House in Dublin, he told the House, a consignment of 6,794 gallons had 4,610 gallons of silent spirit and 2,184 gallons of Irish whiskey. Another consignment of 8,206 gallons had only 299 gallons of Irish whiskey. and at Belfast a 5,115 gallon load contained only 534 gallons of Irish whiskey.

O'Sullivan was proposing that the permits accompanying the dispatch of blended whiskey from Irish bonded stores should carry a distinctive official marking. He argued that such spirits would be accepted by customers as genuine Irish whiskey because of the Custom House permit indicating their Irish port of shipment. He urged that the word 'blended' should be prominently displayed on all such containers in order to remove any possibility of misdescription.

The Limerick M.P. offered to withdraw his amendment asking for the appointment of a Select Committee of Inquiry if the Government would agree to authorise the distinctive markings.

The Chancellor assured the honourable member that the utmost attention would be given to his observations...everything exported would have to have a true name and description.

But behind the bland platitudes remained the immutability of the excise authorities towards any such differentiation or change of method, and there was no existing legislation by which such regulations could be enforced. O'Sullivan's amendment gave rise to considerable debate before being defeated by 145 votes to 69.

The indefatigable Mr. O'Sullivan never ceased to harass the Chancellor, even to the extent of charging the British Government with seeking to destroy the Irish whiskey industry, and reminding him of the increase in duty on Irish whiskey from 2s 8d to 10s between 1852 and 1860, while the increase on English spirits for the same period had been a mere 2s 2d a gallon. But worse than that, he asserted, was the encouragement given to the sale of an inferior article. Mr. O'Sullivan was very well aware, of course, that different scales of duty applied in different parts of the United Kingdom before being made uniform in 1860.

On another occasion he drew the admission that the Chancellor had received petitions signed by 1,982 merchants and spirit retailers in Ireland asking him to put an end to the blending abuses. O'Sullivan then quoted from an advertisement on behalf of a Dublin dealer in which the whiskey blend was described as having been bottled under the immediate supervision of Her Majesty's Customs in Ireland 'and therefore the public had the absolute guarantee of its being pure Dublin whiskey.'

"Does the Government wish to be co-operators in this fraud?" he demanded.

In the 1880s a reverse traffic was in steady operation by which Irish-made grain spirit was being shipped across the channel to be mixed, or blended, with Scotch malt whisky. The distillers of the old Highland malts were equally adamant with their Irish colleagues that the patent still grain spirit was not whisky. In 1887 the Scottish Malt Distillers Association (S.M.D.A.) made a strong protest about this 'adulteration' of their pot still whisky, and challenged the patent still firms to state publicly just what spirits went into their blended products. But the only response from the blenders was a threat to boycott the members of the S.M.D.A. and buy elsewhere if they persisted in their protests.

The blending business boomed, making large profits with very little of the heavy costs and capital investment of the pot still companies whose produce—and capital—lay dormant for years in bonded warehouses, necessarily incurring high rental fees, expensive casking and inevitable losses through evaporation, and of course the crushing price of competition.

But the protests also continued, in press and parliament, and influential medical circles expressed disquiet about the dubious quality of much of the blended spirits. Finally the Government agreed to set up a Select Committee of Commons to inquire 'in the interests of public health' whether certain classes of spirits should be kept in bond for stipulated periods. It would also inquire into the methods of blending British and foreign spirits, and whether the Sale of Food and Drugs Act and the Merchandise Marks Act should apply in the case of British and Foreign spirits 'to indicate the character, origin and state of purity of the products

The Bank of Ireland and former Parliament House, College Green, Dublin.

offered.'

The Committee began its deliberations in the year 1890, and made its report the following year. It decided that the term 'whiskey' had no legal definition, no more than had any other potable spirit, brandy, rum or gin. The Committee did not attempt to make any such legal definition. They recognised the claims made on behalf of spirits made in pot stills and those made in patent stills. They were unable to restrict the use of the term 'whiskey' as long as the spirits used were pure and contained no noxious ingredients. 'The addition of patent still spirits, even when such spirit contains a very small amount of by-products, may be viewed rather as a dilution than an adulteration, as in the case of the addition of water.'

On the question of the compulsory maturing of spirits the Committee maintained a similarly neutral attitude. They would not recommend any increased restrictions on the blending of spirits. The compulsory bonding of all spirits for a certain period was unnecessary, it would only harass trade and would be an unfair burden, they decided.

The futile parliamentary inquiry served only to exacerbate the trade war situation. The new blends constantly arriving on the market, their method of production and comparative quality in relation to traditional Scotch and Irish became a recurring subject of debate and controversy in the editorial and correspondence columns of London newspapers and journals.

As well as some distillers and spirit dealers, publicans in Ireland and Scotland were accused of adulterating whiskey. But despite all the bad publicity brought upon the trade from some quarters, the old-established whiskey companies maintained the high standards of quality on which their reputation rested.

In the early 1900s the Dublin *Evening Mail* ran a series of somewhat sensational articles under the general heading of "Irish Whiskey Frauds" written by an unnamed 'government official well-acquainted with the secrets of this nefarious trade,' according to the editor's note.

The author turned his fire on the silent spirit 'posing first as Irish and then as Scotch whiskey and built into a gigantic business by dealers and traders, leaving the Irish whiskey trade in England and the colonies crippled and almost destroyed.' He had no doubts about where the blame lay. 'The ruin of the Irish whiskey trade in England was brought about by the agency of certain Belfast dealers and blenders who lent themselves to the mean trick of getting over Scotch silent spirit, mixing it with a small quantity of Irish pot still whiskey, blending it, as they termed it, and at the end of a few weeks rushing it across to England as good old Irish pot still whiskey.'

The *Evening Mail* writer recounts some alarming stories about the ingredients used in the manufacture of some types of silent spirit, their ultimate effects on the consumer and the concern they raised among members of the medical profession. To substantiate his allegations he quotes some dubious verse from a contemporary issue of *Punch:*

> Alas, alas poor whiskey,
> That spirit pure and clear,
> Which made its drinker frisky
> Yet left his liver clear.
> How vile adulterations
> Have caused its name to stink,
> Can Irishmen be traitors
> To Ireland's noblest drink?
>
> For the nectarous amber fluid
> That Erin used to send,
> Pure stuff as e'er was brewed,
> We get now a wretched 'blend'.
> For the true potheeny flavour
> And the drink from headache free,
> Now its silent spirit comes along
> And in its train DT.

The anonymous poet continued with more such unmelodious stanzas.

Some investigation into "rumours of spurious compounds passing as whiskey" was made by a Royal Commission appointed in 1896 to inquire into the operation and administration relating to the sale of intoxicating liquor.

Facsimile of a label from *Truths About Whiskey*.

Various witnesses, including medical and police officers, gave evidence of the serious effects brought about by imbibing such drinks. Several samples were taken away for analysis but none of these revealed the presence of deleterious ingredients.

In the course of its Report the Commission said: "It is perhaps not within our province to recommend the bonding of whiskey, nor is it within our power to suggest means whereby such bonding may be sytematically carried out, but we have been so impressed with the evidence of the maddening effects of new spirit, of the pernicious and poisonous consequences of its use on mind and body, that we cannot refrain from pressing upon the notice of the Government the evidence which we have received, and from urging the adoption of some provisions which will mitigate an acknowledged evil."

Chapter 7

Judgement and Appeal

 AN EVENT WHICH had an unexpectedly shattering impact on the great whiskey controversy occurred in November, 1905. It happened in a small North London court-room, where a publican and an off-licence trader were accused of selling an article not of the nature, substance and quality demanded, to wit, whiskey.

The proceedings were brought by Islington Borough Council, a watchful body of representatives who had already achieved success in similar prosecutions in relation to the sale of brandy.

Thomas Wells, publican, of Hornsey, was charged under the Food and Drugs Act in connection with the sale of a bottle of Irish whiskey, and James Davidge, an off-licensee, faced similar charges relating to the sale of Scotch whiskey. The prosecution alleged that the contents of bottles purchased from the defendants' premises contained only ten per cent of genuine pot still Irish and Scotch whiskey and ninety per cent grain spirit, contrary to the description on the labels and not of the quality demanded by the purchaser.

After several sittings and voluminous evidence, much of it technical, including that of the public analyst, the magistrate, Mr. E. Fordham, gave his judgement on the following February 26. He held that the liquor as sold by the defendants, patent spirit blended with a small amount of Irish or Scotch pot still, could not be classified as Irish or Scotch, by which was meant whiskey produced by the pot still method, using malted barley, or a mix of malted and unmalted barley. The spirits sold by the defendants were produced in a patent still from a mash of maize, a grain crop not indiginous to either country, and to which a dash of pot still whiskey had

STILL HOUSE, JOHN'S LANE DISTILLERY.

been added...

In the course of his rather lengthy judgement Mr. Fordham added some personal observations in regard to patent still spirits 'made largely from maize and which, have been sold as whiskey in this country for years past and increasingly taken by an unsuspecting public.'

He censured 'the so-called blenders who dared to concoct and put on the market as Irish or Scotch whiskey raw patent spirit with a mere dash of Irish or Scotch in it.' He imposed a nominal fine on both defendants who, he said, were not the real guilty parties, but who nevertheless had to pay a penalty for a careless infringement of the law.

The result of the case of course stunned the entire blended whiskey trade. The clear implication was that their trade was now illegal. But they just could not accept that a magistrate in a small local court had the power or the right to issue a ruling that could conceivably bring to a halt a vast multi-million pound industry.

Hasty consultations followed, and an appeal was quickly instituted. This time the patent still people saw to it that they had the services of the best legal minds available. But the opposition were also strongly represented.

The appeal opened on May 28, 1906, at the Clerkenwell, London, Quarter Sessions court. After a series of hearings, again mostly technical evidence, stretching on and off over several weeks, the Chairman of the Bench, Mr. W. R. McConnell, rather dolefully announced that a clear decision in the case was not possible, the magistrates were equally divided in their judgement.

Wearily, the distillers and blenders, with their legal advisers reviewed the unsatisfactory position and considered their next move. In effect the Islington ruling had not been set aside. A Royal Commission of Inquiry was seen as the best means of bringing clarity to a confused situation, and both sides agreed to seek Government approval for this course.

It was nearly two years later before the seven-member Commission met, on March 2, 1908, for the first of its thirty-three eventual sittings, during which evidence was taken from more than 100 witnesses. Its final report was issued on July 28, 1909, reversing the findings of the

Islington court and totally vindicating the patent still and blending processes.

The Commission said it found no evidence to show that the form of the still had any necessary relation to the wholesomeness of the spirit produced. The Commission rejected a proposal that the distillers should set out the materials used in the manufacture of potable spirits. In the United Kingdom distilleries, the report said, the trade appeared to be honestly and fairly conducted, with no allegations of fraudulent or semi-fraudulent practice.

The Commission also rejected a proposal for compulsory bonding for a stipulated minimum period, holding that such a regulation would impose an unnecessary burden on particular classes of spirits, bearing in mind that spirits of different character do not mature with equal rapidity.

Finally the Commission gave its definition of whiskey as 'a spirit obtained by distillation from a mash of cereal grains saccharified by the diastase of malt; that Scotch whiskey is whiskey, as above defined, distilled in Scotland; and that Irish whiskey is whiskey, as above defined, distilled in Ireland.'

This, then, was the ultimate ruling, an important and historic decision for the future of Scotch whiskey, and one of immediate and immense relief for the blenders and distillers of the time. Of course it left the pot still distillers, Irish and Scottish disconsolate. There was little in the Commission's report that offered them any comfort.

Chapter 8

Lloyd George and the Irish

 DURING THE NEXT seven years or so the grain spirit trade prospered; new distillers and new dealers appeared on the scene, all intent on getting their share of the profits. Although the Dublin companies were being forced to yield ground in the rich export markets, mainly England and the United States, as a result of the intensive Scottish competition, at least the home market remained firm. Irish whiskey drinkers, like the Scottish highlanders, refused to accept the new lightweight spirit as true whiskey. Some Irish distillers, chiefly in Belfast and Derry, were now manufacturing the new spirit, but most of this was being shipped to Scotland for mixing with pot still.

The outbreak of war in 1914 saw the distilling trade come under increasing restrictions by the British Government. Pot still production was seriously curtailed in 1917 by an order prohibiting the use of the staple ingredient, barley, for any purpose other than the manufacture of food. The use of other ingredients was not affected.

Two years earlier the grain spirit industry suffered its first serious setback with the introduction of a compulsory three-year minimum bonding period for all whiskeys, brought about by Chancellor Lloyd George in his Budget of May, 1915. If the wily Welshman had had his way at that time distilleries, breweries and pubs would have been severely shackled. Not, he was at pains to assure the country, that he was personally endeavouring to promote the cause of temperance, but disciplinary measures were necessary to ensure the success of the war effort on the home front.

In fact, the three-year bonding regulation was a

face-saving compromise for the Chancellor. In his Budget speech he outlined his intention of imposing crippling taxation penalties on all alcoholic spirits. But these extreme measures failed to survive in the parliamentary battle that followed, and in which his most forceful antagonists were members of the Irish Party, a fact that Lloyd George ruefully acknowledged afterwards. The Irish parliamentarians were deeply aware of the threat to the important distilling and brewing industries, as well as farming interests, contained in the Budget proposals.

David Lloyd George is described by the eminent historian, A.J.P. Taylor, in *The Oxford History of England*, as "the nearest thing England has known to a Napoleon, a supreme ruler maintaining himself by individual achievements." The great Liberal leader was a politician of extraordinary resourcefulness and a dictator-like wartime leader of his country. But his seemingly obsessive dislike of alcholic liquor and the entire drink industry led him into clashes with members of his own Party. Perhaps, as he claimed, the stern restrictions he imposed on the trade during the World War I years were dictated by the national interest. He was clearly undaunted by the public wrath his actions aroused.

An adroit manipulator of words Lloyd George saw to it that his speeches made the newspaper headlines. A typical sample of his colourful oratory came at a meeting in Bangor, North Wales, in February 1915, when he told his mesmerised audience: "We are fighting Germany, Austria—and Drink. And as far as I can see the greatest of these deadly foes is Drink!"

In his War Memoirs Lloyd George tells that he viewed with alarm the rapid rise in drink sales in 1915. The menacing evil of drink, he said, slowed down the war effort, caused serious absenteeism and hindered the output of vital munitions. After one bank holiday, he noted, a great number of men failed to report at their work for a whole week.

Almost simultaneously with the Budget the Chancellor introduced his 1915 Drink Bill, on which he had been working for some time. It was an extraordinatry document, aimed at something suspiciously close to total prohibition. The new controls were necessary, he said, in order to give the Government a free hand "unhindered by the immensely powerful influence which the liquor trade has always been able to exert on the politics of this country."

What the Chancellor had in mind was no less than (i) State purchase of all brewery properties in England and Wales; (ii) acquiring control of all branches of the liquor trade that did not come within this category, such as 'free' public-houses and clubs, and (iii) to prohibit, temporarily, retail sales of spirits, but allowing sales of beer below an approved alcoholic strength.

With characteristic zeal he set up special committees to investigate the legal and financial ramifications of these astounding proposals. He was told that the cost to the state of such Draconian action would be a minimum £250 million. He discovered, too, that the practical difficulties of pursuing such a course, particularly as regards such matters as assessing compensation affecting so many diverse interests, would be a lengthy, arduous and complex procedure, requiring a small army of civil servants. There was also the matter of widespread public opposition to such restrictions on human liberty.

The Prime Minister, Mr. Asquith, feared that it might cause trouble within the party.

In view of all these discouraging reports the Chancellor decided on a more limited reform.

During the investigations and negotiations Lloyd George received a wise and witty letter from a Liberal colleague, friend and counsellor, Sir Edwin Montagu, whose opinion he had sought.

"I believe firmly," wrote Sir Edwin, "that, except in cases of apoplexy, shot in the stomach, or congested liver, a man with a moderate amount of alcohol is a better citizen, a better man, a more vigorous individual, than he would be without it. Medical evidence shows that alcohol is a poison, and like so many other poisons, in moderation it is beneficial, and total abstinence seems to me to be morally as great a weakness as insobriety.

"I cannot find myself in agreement with you that there is any evidence that drink has hampered us in this war on any such substantial scale as would call for heroic remedies."

Sir Edwin suggested that absenteeism was due not so much to the effects of drinking as the effects of overtime working on men unused to working long hours. Overtime working, he contended, was economically bad. He reminded the Chancellor also that drink receipts had risen considerably mainly because of the Chancellor's own taxation imposts and the increased costs of raw materials and labour. Closing the pubs, he said, would be an unjust penalty on men who work under very trying conditions.

Having decided, reluctantly, to abandon his attempts to buy over the entire liquor trade, and prohibit the sale of spirits, Lloyd George then proceeded to draw up measures to ensure a more effective state control of the drink busines. A government White Paper was circulated outlining the amount of time lost in vital industrial areas and the necessity for imposing wartime restrictions on excessive drinking.

Despite vigorous opposition the Bill was carried, and a Central Control Board to deal with Liquor Traffic was set up. The Board was given the power to close, in any area under its control, any licensed premises or club, to regulate hours of opening, to prohibit the sale or supply of any class of intoxicant, to impose conditions and restrictions for licensed premises, or to prohibit trading.

Although most of these restrictive practices were repealed or otherwise fell into disuse with the end of the war, the last vestiges only disappeared in 1975. This occurred with the sale by the Government of the last of the state-owned pubs in Carlisle.

The stern measures in the wartime Bill also made illegal such traditional convivialities as treating and standing rounds. In London pub trading was narrowed down to Sunday hours.

In his Budget speech a shocked House of Commons heard Chancellor Lloyd George announce that he proposed to double the tax on spirits, which would raise it to 29s 6d per proof gallon, and raise the maximum permissable dilution of spirits from 25 to 35 degrees underproof. He would also quadruple the tax on wines and impose a graded surtax on beer.

These proposals raised a storm of protest inside and outside Parliament. "The Irish Party was particularly angry because of the big distilling interests in that country," Lloyd George observed afterwards, "and I was compelled to abandon, for the time being, these proposed taxes."

With typical candour, Lloyd George, in his memoirs, confessed that "this reasonable scheme encountered very bitter opposition, and in further proposals for the general discouragement of drinking I was at first compelled to swallow an almost complete defeat."

The doughty Welsh fighter, badly scarred, did emerge with one consoling point, prohibition of the sale of whiskey under three years old, a measure aimed at stopping the marketing of the newer and more fiery spirit. This compromise measure was readily conceded by the Irish Party. In fact the Irish pot still interests regarded it as a significant achievement, as a minimum three-year bonding or maturation period was a quality requirement traditionally observed by them. The Irish Party spokesman indeed had urged the Chancellor to drop his penal taxation proposals in favour of the compulsory bonding regulations.

The new measure, which became law as the Immature Spirits (Restriction) Act, came as a bitter blow to the Coffey still operators, many of whom sold off the spirit almost straight from the still and had no warehousing facilities. It meant, in effect, a three-year setback in marketing operations, a crushing penalty that put many distillers out of business.

It did not, of course, seriously jeopardise the affairs of the reputable and old-established Scotch blended whisky firms who aged their product, and indeed the new regulation could be seen as a blessing in disguise by promoting a more consistent quality for blended whisky.

Soon afterwards Lloyd George was appointed Minister of Munitions, and in due course he announced that all patent still distilleries would be temporarily appropriated by the Government and turned over to making spirit for explosives. It was decided that the pot stills were not suitable for this work, but production was slowed down by further curtailment of essential materials for brewing and distilling.

John Power & Sons' Distillery, Johns Lane Dublin, 1878.

Chapter 9

Law and Disorder

 EARLY IRISH chronicles have it that an Irish bishop sent a cask of *usquebagh* to Queen Elizabeth I. It is recorded that Her Majesty liked it and ordered more. Whatever motives may have prompted the bishop the gesture was certainly a marvellous publicity exercise. The word about the Irish *aqua vitae* got around. Scarcely a hundred years later King Charles II got the idea that he could swell the royal coffers by imposing an excise tax on the stuff. Fourpence a gallon would be enforced, he decided. This move didn't find much favour with the suppliers and consumers, many of whom found devious ways of avoiding the extra penalty. Illegal distilling has been with us ever since.

Songs and stories and legends abound about the exploits of the poitín men down through the ages. All, or most of them, one suspects, were composed or invented by balladeers and seanachies who were temporarily under the influence of 'the good old mountain dew.' The plain truth is far removed from the romanticism of sodden songsters. Some of the old poitín may indeed have been worthy of the distiller's craft, but then it was also said of the illegal spirit that 'its only recommendation is that it has not paid the Crown any duty.' One notable authority, the late Brendan Behan, firmly dismissed the moonshine. 'Potheen is just murder. It's the end, and you can take it from me, for I have had a wide enough experience of it,' he comments in his book, *Brendan Behan's Island* (Hutchinson, 1962).

Illicit distilling in Ireland reached virtually uncontrollable proportions during the 18th and early 19th centuries, a widespread rural industry that defied all the strictures and all the weight of the imperial establishment. Hordes of excise men, backed up by the military, failed to suppress the traffic. There were violent clashes. Men were killed, kidnapped and tortured because of it. Corruption, cruelty and injustice fanned the winds of open rebellion.

Whiskey smuggling was an economic necessity in parts of rural Ireland, particularly along the western seaboard. Smallholders rented land to the smugglers, or turned to illicit distilling themselves if they failed to find an economic market for their grain.

Among the weapons of suppression employed by the revenue authorities was the imposition of fines on entire towns or parishes where a poitín still, or even part of a still, was found. Such evidence was deemed to be conclusive by the excise authorities who had absolute power in the matter. No specific charge was required, no defence was heard and no appeal allowed. Every adult person in the parish was forced to pay his share.

Such a harshly unjust system inevitably bred corruption. Informers were encouraged and bribed to assist the authorities. The communal fines system, introduced in 1783, eventually had the effect of reducing significantly the smuggling traffic. Having to some extent achieved its aim, and in the face of widespread protests in parliament and in public about the injustice and unfairness of the system, the practice was discontinued in the year 1810.

But of course the wily poitín men saw this cessation of hostilities as the signal for a return to normal trading conditions and they promptly resumed business. The resultant upsurge in the traffic brought about the resumption of the fines system in 1814, when even harsher penalties were imposed on the local populations. For a first offence the fine was £25, for a second offence £40, and £60 for each succeeding occasion.

Half of this booty was paid to the excise officer and his assistant making the find. There was also an increased financial inducement to informers to betray their neighbours. The excise men of the time were badly paid, poorly equipped and had little training. Few of them were adverse to bending the rules and using their badge of authority in order to augment their meagre official salary. The deliberate planting of parts of previously seized stills was an obvious form of conspiracy. Small

Gardai proudly display a selection of seized equipment.

landowners were frequently intimidated by threats of exposure into parting with money or property. The parish fine was not imposed where any local inhabitant gave information leading to the conviction of any person or persons.

Our old friend Aeneas Coffey gives us a revealing account of the conditions in those bad old days. In 1818, while serving as a zealous excise officer in Co. Donegal, he published a pamphlet in reply to one which had been issued by the Rev. Edward Chichester. The reverend gentleman, who also lived in north Donegal was firmly on the side of the local poitín manufacturers and felt so wrathful at the behaviour of the excise authorities and their minions that he was incensed into publishing and distributing his pamphlet in London under the uncompromising title of *Oppressions and Cruelties of Revenue Officers in Ireland*.

He roundly attacked what he called 'the universal corruption and collusion of excise men, maintained and defended by their superiors in office and tolerated by the Board of Excise.'

Aeneas Coffey as an honourable Irishman no doubt must have seen much that was wrong with the excise administration of the time, and, having reached the high post of Inspector General, we must assume that he had quite a lot to do with the subsequent gradual reformation and improvement of that body. But in the meantime he was a dedicated upholder of the regulations as they then existed, and he could not allow the Rev. Edward Chichester to pour forth his scathing denunciation of his profession without replying for the defence.

Coffey sternly pointed out that in a preceding year more than two million gallons of illicit spirits were manufactured, most of this in Co. Donegal, and with an excise duty of tenpence a gallon, this was defrauding the state on a vast scale and could not be tolerated.

He said that in the barony of Innishowen alone there were, at a moderate estimate, about 800 private stills turning out thousands of gallons of illegal spirits for distribution to neighbouring counties, as well as dispatching large quantities to Dublin and Belfast, and even exporting to Scotland, from where they received quantities of barley in part exchange.-

Coffey claimed that whole areas of North Donegal

The widespread smuggling of whiskey found a ready market at the Donnybrook Fair where "during the merry month of August it was a famed spot for drollery and drunkedness".

were covered with illicit distilling apparatuses, up to within a mile of Derry city. Excise officers entered these areas at the risk of their lives, he said, and even an armed military bodyguard was insufficient protection. Later, in testimony before a commission of inquiry investigating illicit distilling, Coffey said he could state instances of revenue officers being barbarously assaulted and even murdered. Many officials were kidnapped by smugglers to prevent them giving evidence in court, he said.

Both Coffey and Chichester related accounts of armed clashes between the smugglers and the excise men with their military escorts, with frequent casualties on both sides. Coffey described the situation as one of 'outrage and rebellion.'

The Rev. Chichester claimed that the peasants were justified in protecting their livelihood in the face of injustice and persecution, and he accused the excise men's armed bodyguard of using unwarranted force. He defended his people on the grounds that the miserable tracts of rock and bog on which they subsisted were incapable of yielding any other form of sustenance.

Coffey held that the military were present only to assist the officials in carrying out their duties, such as the collection of fines. To show how frustrating this task could be he recalled an occasion when the troops moved in to assist the chief constable to collect the penal dues, only to find that the lawman refused to act. It transpired that he was a native of the locality and had been tried in an excise court for smuggling. No one else could be persuaded to deputise!

The late 18th and early 19th centuries were the boom period for whiskey smuggling and a bad time for the legitimate trade. The situation was brought about chiefly by an atrociously misguided piece of legislation. This was the Distilling Act of 1779, which was drawn up by the revenue authorities in the hope of checking the widespread evasion of the payment of spirit duties by distillery owners.

It introduced a complicated system of imposing a minimum payment on every still, calculated on size and capacity. It was based on the assumption that each still, fully loaded, could be worked a minimum number of times over each period of 28 days.

But the revenue people, after a time, were not satisfied

that they were getting the maximum return, and so they gradually raised the minimum number of still workings. Speed of operation thus became the criterion, with product quality a lesser factor. It was inevitable that many distillers found the situation and the strain intolerable, and were forced to close down.

Those who remained in business could do so only by indulging in the widespread corruption which the new regulations helped to foster. Collusion betwen distillery owners and excise officials was commonplace, and little attempt was made to hide the practice. Excise gaugers, or assessors, demanded and received private payments in order to cover up any deficiencies that might arise under the revenue regulations.

And the effects of those regulations were indeed crippling. In 1779, when the Act was drawn up, there were 1,000 or more legal distilleries in Ireland, most of them small concerns, but by 1790 the number had dropped to about 250.

It was not until 1823 that the still charge system was abolished with the introduction of more enlightened legislation. The Act of 1823, which still forms the basis for most of today's licensing regulations, sensibly ordained that duty would be assessed on the actual amount of spirit produced in the distillery and on the strength of the spirit. It allowed the distiller to concentrate on turning out a more carefully made and more palatable whiskey. In addition to taking the pressure off the manufacturer, the spirit duty was halved to 2s per proof gallon, and a yearly distilling licence fee of £10 introduced. These new regulations gave a great impetus to the distilling industry, restoring efficiency and confidence.

They also lessened the competition from the poitín men, many of whom found it worth their while at this period to turn 'legit.' It was impossible to eradicate illegal distilling completely, and probably always will be, in spite of new measures introduced over the succeeding years. One of the most important of these was the establishment of a revenue police force to deal with the problem. The experiment was not successful, and in 1857 the force was disbanded and their duties were handed over to the local constabulary.

The constabulary had not previously been required to

The military frequently accompanied the excise men in carrying out their duties.
This barracks is at Ship Street, Dublin.

pursue the poitín merchants, except on special occasions, and they were reluctant to accept the additional responsibilities. However, they finally agreed, and it was from about this time that illegal distilling began to recede as a serious threat to law and order—and to the national economy. But old traditions linger, and even today the Garda Siochána still make the nostalgic capture of a portable distillery in the remote countryside.

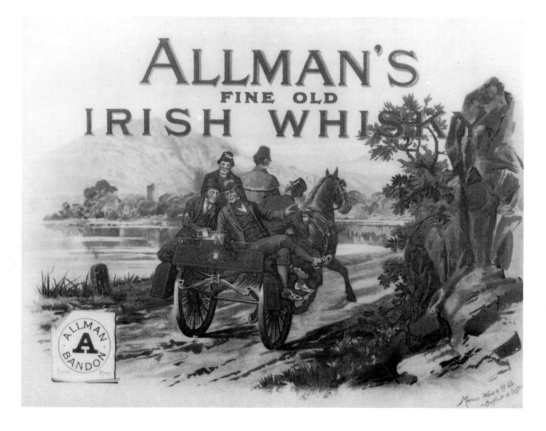

Chapter 10

Smugglers' Tales

 THAT DISTINGUISHED 19th century English historian of the distilling industry, Alfred Barnard, who made an extensive tour in Ireland, also gives us an interesting insight into this period.

Poitín was regarded throughout Ulster as superior to much of the legal produce, which was disparagingly referred to as 'parliament whiskey.' This preference extended to people of rank, who gladly paid high prices for 'the good stuff.' Legal whiskey sold at approximately 7s a gallon, while poitín prices varied from 3s to as much as 9s a gallon.

Barnard had quite a high regard for the poitín men, small farmers forced into the illegal trade by economic necessity. The old smugglers, he said, were expert at their job and were the forerunners of the distilling industry in Ireland. They were careful to select a locality where the pure mountain stream flowed over moss and peat to manufacture spirits of some distinction, made from high quality malted barley. Many of them later went into the business legally.

Although Barnard defended the smugglers' operations as 'a justifiable evasion of undue laws,' he also regretted the necessity for such illegal trading which, he said, was injurious, not only to the agriculture and revenue of the country, but also harmful to the morals and peaceful habits of the community.

Barnard tells us that in the year 1806, out of 11,400,000 gallons of spirits made in Ireland, 3,800,000 of these were produced by illicit manufacturers. In the years 1811 to 1813 almost 20,000 illegal stills were destroyed by the revenue authorities and the military. In regard to community fines on parishes and townlands he said that over a seven-year period the average annual sum totalled just over £50,000. In 1814 the fines imposed on County Donegal alone amounted to £18,000.

Alfred Barnard took a close interest in the activities of the illegal manufacturers, both in Ireland and Scotland. He even won the confidence of the smugglers to the extent that he was allowed to visit some of the illicit operators to observe their methods. He relates a few bizarre stories concerning the artfulness of the smugglers in outwitting the excise people, as well as their ruthlessness in defying the dictates of the law. For some of these versions he relies on the earlier writings of Samuel Morewood, a former excise official and, like Barnard, an assiduous historian of the trade. As for the authenticity of these smugglers' tales, well, who knows now? Certainly, the diligence of these two writers in their task of investigating and recording encourages the assumption that at least they contain some substance of truth.

The astuteness of the moonshine men is well typified in the story of the dedicated excise man and the vanishing smuggler. Repeatedly the official saw the peasant figure leading his horse across the lonely stretch of ground at dead of night. A substantial sack was thrown across the horse's back. But as the official watched, both man and horse seemed suddenly to disappear in the darkness. One moonlit night the determined official followed his quarry at a safe distance. But again the disappearing trick took place. The lawman made a careful note of the spot, and early next day, with military assistance he set out for the mysterious rendezvous.

He found everything serene and silent, with not a clue to the mystery. The poor man began to worry that he might be having delusions. The ground appeared to be unmarked as his eyes searched anxiously around. He saw some brambles loosely scattered about, and as he kicked through them he found some loose sods underneath. As the men pulled away the sods they came upon a trap door. This led to a small cavern, at the bottom of which the party looked upon a complete miniature distillery, supplied by a subterranean stream. Further excavation revealed a winding tube which conveyed the smoke from the still to a house some distance off where it was funnelled into the chimney.

Test marketing a new secret brew.

There were tales of excise officers being kidnapped to prevent them giving evidence. At the approach of the Donegal Assizes in 1803 an officer stationed at Dunfanaghy, and due to testify at an illicit distilling case, was seized, blindfolded and carried off by a body of men. He was taken to the Aran isle of Inishmaan, where he was confined, threatened and even put to work at a secret still. After thirteen days he was again blindfolded, taken by boat to the mainland and carried far inland. His blindfold was removed, and he was pushed forward and warned not to look back, and left to make his way home.

Another account tells of an officer seized from his home in the middle of the night and, only partially dressed, put into a sack up to his chin and thrown across the back of a horse. He was brought to a lake some distance away, and the terrified man heard his captors deliberate whether they should tie a stone to the sack and toss him into the lake, or give him a more lingering death. They decided to move on to a mountainous region, where the official was subjected to insults, privation and threat of violent death.

Meanwhile, at the Assizes when the illicit distilling case came up for hearing, the judge rightly suspected that the accused parties were accessories to the kidnap outrage. With menace in his voice he announced that unless the abducted official was liberated and returned to his home forthwith, he would impose sentences as would forever put out of the prisoners' heads the thought of any other such offence. The stern warning was duly heeded. The kidnap victim was again tied into the sack and surreptitiously conveyed back to within a few miles of his home.

Most of Alfred Barnard's stories about the funnier side of the smuggling game seem to come from Scotland. One of these is a classic of its kind.

It concerns one Magnus Eunson who lived on the Isle of Orkney, an upright citizen, a church verger—and a most resourceful smuggler. Only a man like Magnus would have thought of keeping his store of illicit liquor under the church pulpit.

One of his henchmen informed Magnus of hearing that a newly-arrived excise officer planned to carry out a search of the church as part of his drive to track down the source of the illegal spirit which had such a wide

The whole family became involved in distilling *Poitín*.

popularity in the neighbourhood. Magnus was outraged at the news. "How dare they desecrate the church in this fashion?" he thundered. Nevertheless Magnus arranged to have the hoard discreetly transferred from the church to his home.

What hurt Magnus Eunson most was the thought that one of his trusted associates had betrayed him and turned informer. The raiding party carried out their search of the church, and of course, much to their disgust, found nothing. As Magnus had anticipated, after the abortive search the excise men went straight to his house.

There they found Magnus Eunson, his family and friends in a room without furniture or floor covering, all on their knees, sobbing, wailing and praying. In the centre of the room a large white cloth covered what the startled excise men took to be a coffin. Eunson, a bible in his hand, looked up from his reading to give a sad greeting to the visitors and pointed to the coffin to indicate the family bereavement. One of the mourners turned to the leader of the excise party and sorrowfully murmured just one word: "Smallpox!" As the horrified excise men turned and ran, the 'mourning' ceremony came to a successful and jubilant conclusion.

In another tale from the Highland glens an officer kept an isolated house under observation, convinced that it was used for illicit whisky manufacturing. Early one morning he watched the house, and saw the men leaving for work in the fields. Cautiously he made his approach, listened for a while and then pushed the door open and entered. Inside he found the equipment he suspected as well as some of its produce.

The sole occupant of the house at this time was a woman, a lady of formidable proportions who loomed large over the smaller official. Having identified himself, the woman inquired if he was alone. He assured her he was quite alone. "And nobody saw ye come in?" "No, ma'am, nobody."

"Praises be for that," exclaimed the large woman, as she rolled up her sleeves and advanced menacingly toward the excise man. "And be the holy, nobody will see ye goin' oot aither!"

In its futile attempts to put an end to the activities of the Highland whisky smugglers the English government once offered a £5 reward for information on the location of secret stills, a situation of which the resourceful nomadic distillers took full advantage. When their most expensive item of equipment, the coiled copper pipe known as the worm, or condenser, became worn out they dismantled the apparatus, carefully leaving some parts of the old still intact, and promptly notified the authorities of finding an illicit still. Gratefully accepting the state reward for their diligence they went happily off to purchase a new copper coil and other items, and were quickly back in business with up-to-date equipment.

Few people, even the law enforcers, can resist the exciting temptation to drink from the forbidden cup at times. The story is told—and like most of the moonshiners' tales, with no guarantee of its veracity—of the two young Gardai out for a day's wildfowling in the West of Ireland some years ago who came across a secreted five-gallon keg of poitin. They conveyed it to the residence of one of them, where they bottled about three gallons of the concoction, and poured a similar amount of water into the container. Then they brought the booty into their local garda station and promptly claimed the going reward of the time for their capture.

The station sergeant commended the boys on their find and then quietly invited a neighbouring sergeant colleague to come and fill himself a bottle or two of the stuff. This was done and the keg was again surreptitiously topped up with water. The superintendent was then duly notified of the find, but before saying goodbye to their prize the two boys that evening decided to bottle another few pints. The super, an ardent teetotaller, arrived next day, complimented the pair of lads on their conscientious application to duty and promised to recommend them for the reward. He then formally emptied out the watery contents of the keg.

Chapter 11

Daniel O'Connell and Father Mathew

 THE EXPLANATION for the upsurge in illicit distilling during the late 18th and early 19th century might be found in the history books for the period. The poitín proliferation must certainly have been brought about primarily by economic necessity, but it also could have been seen as a gesture of defiance by an oppressed people against an alien establishment. Ireland was a lawless state, deprived and rebellious, and was still emerging from the blackest period in her history.

Older people still talked about the worst excesses of the Penal Laws, that infamous chain of coercive legislation, which lasted well into the 19th century and whose scars still lay across the land. This was Ireland's dark age, when the native population had to suffer the forcible suppression of their religion, their education and their cherished traditions.

The right of entry to the legal profession, parliament or any form of public life was denied to the native Irish. Restrictions were placed on ownership of property and farms; industry and agriculture were frustrated by repressive English laws and embargoes. The peasant people were classed as being lazy and shiftless, an unjust opprobrium considering that neither the opportunity nor the incentive to work was made available, except in the more menial occupations. Evictions for non-payment of rents were frequent occurrences. There was little protection in the law or the courts, where harsh sentences were meted out for trivial offences.

Repressive rule invariably breeds rebellious tendencies. Secret societies emerged in the Ireland of the late 18th century, like the Whiteboys, formed in Co. Limerick around 1760, which sought to exact retribution

An enthusiastic crowd watch the laying of the foundation stone for the
O'Connell Monument, Dublin 1864.

from unjust rural landlords. The year 1791 brought into being the Society of United Irishmen, founded by Theobald Wolfe Tone and his Presbyterian colleagues in Belfast. It had the objects of achieving civil, religious and political liberty, hopefully by constitutional means but which almost inevitably assumed a revolutionary character and brought about the Insurrection of 1798, a bitterly-fought uprising which was eventually suppressed with much ferocity by the English armies.

The dominant figure in the early 19th century was of course Daniel O'Connell, the Liberator. The brilliant Kerry-born barrister, member of parliament, Lord Mayor and people's champion, was also a physically impressive figure, but his conservative and pacifist outlook ensured that he would never be short of more militant opponents on the nationalist side. O'Connell's main achievement was in steering the Catholic Emancipation Bill through a reluctant parliament in 1829. Twelve years later he became Dublin's first Catholic Lord Mayor since the reign of King James II.

O'Connell had a brief association with the licensed trade when he assisted his youngest son, Daniel junior, to acquire a brewery in James's Street, Dublin, for the production of O'Connell's Ale, a brew which enjoyed considerable popularity.

Whatever about the product itself, the business venture was not wholly successful. After a few years O'Connell's Brewery was taken over by the manager, John Brennan, and Daniel junior devoted himself to a career in politics. Brennan changed the name of the enterprise to the Phoenix Brewery and continued to brew and advertise O'Connell's Ale. The brewery was eventually absorbed into the Guinness complex in 1909. When the Phoenix closed, the brewing of O'Connell's Ale was carried on by John D'Arcy and Son Ltd. at the Anchor Brewery in Usher Street. The labels used for O'Connell's Ale now incorporated a representation of the monument to the Liberator in Sackville (later O'Connell) Street. D'Arcy ceased trading in the mid-1920s and the firm of Watkins Jameson & Pim in turn carried on the brewing of O'Connell's Ale. This company changed the label design to one carrying a vignette of the Liberator.

Daniel O'Connell junior was a member of the licensed trade association of the period and held the office of committee chairman. The trade association was formed in 1817 by a Dublin vintner, James Lube, and some of his colleagues who were alarmed at the abuses that prevailed in the trade, particularly the manner in which drink licences were being handed out, and the evils of shebeens, places where illicit spirits could be bought and consumed.

In an article in the trade journal, *The Licensed Vintner*, commemorating, in 1967, the 150th anniversary of the publicans' association, Michael Gill wrote:

"The early part of the nineteenth century was an exciting time in Dublin. The Irish Parliament was gone, revolution was rife. The city was full of soldiers who had looted half the world in the wars of Napoleon. Wine from Spain and Portugal and brandy from France, which had sustained the Anglo-Normans for generations, were in short supply and of inferior quality. The native brew had come into its own.

"The Irish nation had got through 11 million gallons of native whiskey and about 200 million gallons of beer. Peace and unemployment followed the English victory at Waterloo. Tradesmen began to fight bitterly the fall in wages, and James Lube of Ship Street called the tavern-keepers of Dublin together to discuss the protection of their interests.

"There had been several attempts before to get a trade association started, but lack of funds had defeated the founders. The old guild, the Cooks' and Vintners' Guild, which had survived for 400 years in Cook Street, off Winetavern Street, had fallen into the hands of wholesalers and politicians, and the Penal Laws had prevented Catholics from taking a prominent part in any of their deliberations. The Grocers' Bill, in 1817, was going through Parliament, and so many of the so-called Rotten Boroughs were controlled by publicans who bought and sold the seats in Parliament on behalf of their customers, feeling that their combined influence should be able to protect their livelihoods..."

The new licensed trade association gave formidable and valuable support to Daniel O'Connell in his public life, but some time later a quarrel arose and O'Connell turned his back on the association, and indeed became a strong advocate of temperance. Drunkenness and poverty were reaching alarming proportions. In a

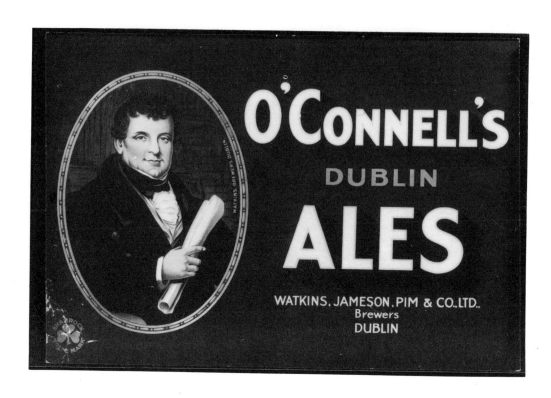

parliamentary inquiry in 1834 'into the extent, causes and consequences of drunkenness in the United Kingdom' evidence was given that in Dublin the number of licences to sell spirits rose from 868 in 1824 to 1,714 in 1828. There was also 'extensive private distilling,' it was noted.

Temperance societies were formed in the cities and towns to combat excessive drinking and to campaign against the lax regulations which failed to control the evil. But it was not until 1838 that the anti-drink crusade began to assume national proportions, with the appearance on the scene of Father Theobald Mathew, the Capuchin Friar from Cork, who by his dynamic and self-sacrificing zeal turned the tide within a few years with his total abstinence campaign. Father Mathew stormed the country, addressing huge public meetings and restoring resolute self-respect in a people deep in despair and degradation. In two visits to Dublin in August and September, 1840, he preached in the Pro-Cathedral and other churches, and also addressed a vast concourse of people from a platform erected at the Custom House. In the two visits he was said to have enrolled over 75,000 in his Total Abstinence Movement.

But the Apostle of Temperance was not without his outspoken critics. Walter Thomas Meyler, a Dublin tea and wine merchant, and a keen observer of the local scene, published a booklet which he called *St. Catherine's Bells*, some years after Fr. Mathew's death in 1856. In it Meyler expressed his dislike of the extremes of intemperance and total abstention. He insisted that the Father Mathew crusade was only further injuring the plight of the people by hitting the economy and putting workers out of jobs. Only by improving the wretched conditions of the underprivileged would the evils of drunkenness be eliminated.

"His (Fr. Mathew's) disciples spread the monomania like a simona over the land," wrote Meyler. "Brewers, grocers and country shopkeepers were paralysed, thousands fled the country and their creditors. About one hundred distilleries and breweries had to close down, their owners and workers reduced to destitution..."

But whatever about the effect on the economy, the remarkable Father Mathew rallied the people of Ireland as no political figure had ever done, and he succeeded in

reducing the consumption of alcohol more than any legislation ever could. In 1838, when he undertook his mission, there were approximately 21,300 taverns or drink outlets around the country. In less than six years this figure was down to 13,500. As a matter of comparison, the number of fully licensed premises in the Republic of Ireland in 1978 was about 10,500, serving a population of just over three million.

As a result of Father Mathew's total abstinence crusade, several new temperance societies came into prominence around the country. In his book, *An Apostle of Catholic Dublin*, an account of the life of the saintly Dublin priest, Fr. Henry Young (1786-1869), Rev. Myles V. Ronan gives some illustrative details of this period.

The most spectacular event was the huge temperance rally held on St. Patrick's Day in 1841, when all the temperance units in Dublin and surrounding areas paraded in a colourful cavalcade of bands and banners through the city to Phoenix Park, an occasion which brought out over 200,000 people, according to the *Catholic Luminary*, a local journal of the time. The parade was headed by the president of the Metropolitan Temperance Association, Rev. Andrew O'Connell, pastor of SS Michael and John's parish, who rode "in a splendid carriage, drawn by four white steeds, driven by postillions and proceeded by couriers dressed in buff breeches, blue spencers and skull caps with tassels of gold.'

Some of the temperance associations had memberships numbering several thousands, and they promoted various sporting and social functions. Daniel O'Connell was guest of honour at a temperance festival held in the Rotunda.

The predominantly "loyal" outlook of the leaders of these parochial temperance groups was striking. Reports of the various functions constantly refer to the banners carrying such slogans as "God Save the Queen," and "Long Live Prince Albert." The "loyal toast," with appropriate beverages, was evidently an essential formality, while the bands invariably played "a selection of loyal and Irish tunes."

Dr. Ronan gives an interesting account of the church of SS Michael and John, which stands in Lower

Exchange Street, close to the River Liffey. The church is built on the site of one of Dublin's most noted 18th century theatres, in Smock Alley, which later became West Essex Street. The auditorium of the theatre became the church's burial vaults. Almost adjoining Smock Alley, in Fishamble Street, stood another celebrated proscenium of the time, Neal's Music Hall, whose name should not be confused with the rather less dignified music-hall era of a later period. The Fishamble Street venue aspired more to the status of concert hall and acquired distinction as the stage from which George Frederick Handel's 'Messiah' was given to the world. The composer introduced his great oratorio to the Dublin audience on April 13, 1742, during Holy Week. Incidentally Handel died in London on the same date in 1759, which happened to be Good Friday, the seventeenth anniversary of the first performance of the 'Messiah.'

The old Smock Alley theatre building was purchased in the year 1790 by a Dublin brewer, James Farrelly, of No. 4 Merrion Square East, who owned a brewery at Black Pitts, and who converted the theatre into a warehouse and stores. In 1811 he handed over the now decaying building to the local parish priest, Dr. Michael Blake, who was seeking a site for a new parish church. The price, we are told, was £1,600. The splendid new church was opened in 1815.

Dr. Blake installed a tolling bell in his new parish church, in defiance of the existing penal code. It was the first such public bell in any Catholic place of worship in 300 years, and its installation aroused the wrath of the local Orange establishment. One of them, a Councillor Carleton, instituted proceedings in the King's Bench against the parish priest. But Dr. Blake secured the advocacy of Daniel O'Connell and, after consultations, the councillor withdrew his complaint.

Chapter 12

Licensing Laws and Iniquities

 THE FIRST STATUTE governing the sale of intoxicating liquor in Ireland was enacted in the year 1635, during the reign of Charles I. It followed 136 years after the first such enactment for England, when Henry VII was the ruling monarch. The reasons why it was necessary to exercise some state control over the Irish liquor trade are set forth in the preamble:

"Forasmuch as it is found by daily experience that many mischiefs and inconveniences doe arise from the excessive number of ale-houses, from the erection of them in woods, bogges and other unfit places, and many of them not in towneships but dispersedly, in dangerous places and kept by unknown persons not under taken, for whereby many times they become resceptacles for rebels and other malefactors, and harbours for gamesters and other idle, disordered and unprofitable livers, and that those who keep these ale-houses for the most part are not fitted or furnished to lodge or entertain travellers in any decent manner: For the redresse of these inconveniences and many other mischiefes dayly observed to grow by the course now held and to reduce those needlesse multitudes of ale-houses to a fewer number, to more fit persons, and to more convenient places."

The Act ordained that no one was to keep any ale-house or tippling-house or sell any ale or beer by retail unless licensed by commissioners appointed from time to time. The licences were to be granted annually in the first quarter sessions after Easter by at least two commissioners to persons of good character, for a proper number of houses in convenient places, and were to last for one year. The houses had to provide accommodation, and sell provisions at reasonable rates to travellers. The licence duty would cost five shillings.

It is interesting to note that in the report of the exhaustive royal commission inquiry into the sale of intoxicating liquor in the United Kingdom 1896-99, in the section relating to Ireland, the then Solicitor General in Ireland, Mr. Dunbar Barton, reiterated his opinion that this original statute, subsequently repealed, contained and embodied almost all the principal provisions of subsequent licensing legislation in Ireland, and that the main principles of the Act relating to the licensed trade in Ireland had hardly been improved.

Nevertheless every government in every age since then has contributed its series of additions and amendments to these basic principles, so that today we have a confused and puzzling labyrinth of licensing legislation.

As Mr. Gladstone said in 1868: "So great are the difficulties and so anomalous our licensing laws that every attempt hitherto made to reduce them to something like order or principle has failed."

And as Mr. Justice Fitzgerald observed in the course of a judgment in 1877: "The provisions of the numerous statutes which regulate licences for the use of intoxicating liquors in Ireland are so complex, uncertain and contradictory that it is difficult to carry them into effect, or to reach the meaning and intention of the legislature."

It was not until sixty years had elapsed after the passing of the first statute that a law relating to the hours of closing was laid down. This simply stated that all licensed premises must remain closed during the hours of divine service on Sundays.

An Act of 1791, passed in the Irish Parliament, made it illegal to give liquor in lieu of wages, and ordered that wages could no longer be paid out in a public-house. Also any debt over 20 shillings incurred for the sale of spirits on credit was no longer recoverable in law.

The spirit grocer licence, a regulation peculiar to Ireland, and one which led to so much mischief and damage, was also introduced in 1791. It allowed that grocers in Dublin might be licensed by collectors of excise to sell spirits by retail, in quantities of not less than one pint, for consumption off the premises. The naive thinking behind this Act was that it would spare women the moral danger of having to enter public houses to purchase spirits. Instead, it led many of them into alcoholism.

The Spirit Grocers Act of 1818 repealed the previous Acts relating to grocers, and laid down that any grocer, in any place, might take out a licence from the Excise to retail spirits and other liquors, for consumption off the premises, on payment of the same duty as innkeepers. The Revenue Act of 1825 further laid down that a person duly licensed to "deal in or sell coffee, tea, cocoa-nuts, chocolate or pepper" shall be deemed a grocer and be allowed to take out the licence to retail spirits in any quantity not exceeding two quarts at one time, to be consumed off the premises. No certificate was required.

The spirit grocers were largely confined to Dublin and Belfast, where they increased rapidly in numbers because of the ease with which licences could be obtained. In evidence at the Royal Commission, a Belfast police District Inspector denounced the spirit grocer licence as "the greatest curse in the licensed trade." They demoralised the women and led to an illicit trade which was almost impossible to stop, he said.

Judge Orr, County Court Judge for Down and part of Antrim, also before the Commission, said spirit grocers were the greatest evil in Ireland. Much illicit drinking went on and many women became addicted to the practice of drinking behind screens of biscuit boxes. The law relating to spirit grocers was absurd, said Judge Orr. Anybody who could not get a publican's licence took out a spirit grocer's licence. They did not require a magistrate's certificate, and the licence was not endorsable, even in the event of conviction for selling drink consumed on the premises.

Despite the anomalies and abuses in the system the spirit grocer establishments were not abolished until 1910. The spirit grocer should not be confused with the publican grocer, a trade combination that flourished in Ireland until the 1930s.

In Dublin in the early 19th century anybody seeking a publican's licence had to obtain an order from the Lord Mayor, who also had the power to annul a licence. This authority was subsequently withdrawn from the Lord Mayor and confined to Divisional Justices.

The Licensing (Ireland) Act of 1837 gave the Recorder, sitting in Dublin, Belfast and the principal towns at the quarter sessions, sole authority to grant or refuse publicans' licences. Renewal of the licence could be obtained directly from the Excise on the production of a certificate signed by six householders. Three years later this regulation was amended to include the approval of the District Inspector of Police.

In the smaller towns, grant renewal and transfer of public-house licences were dealt with by justices assembled at quarter sessions under the chairmanship of the County Court Judge. This system was roundly condemned in the report of the 1899 Commission of Inquiry, where some astounding accounts of malpractice in the licensing administration were related.

The Commissioners found that the number of licensed houses throughout all Ireland was excessive and out of all proportion to the necessities of the population, and a large reduction in their numbers was, in the highest degree, desirable. It is noted that they also called for a large reduction in the number of public houses in England and Wales.

The Commission recorded that "the ordinary people of Ireland are a sober people except when they visit the small towns for fairs or markets. In these towns the congestion of public houses is almost incredible."

It was calculated that, taking one public-house as supplying adequate accommodation for a hundred families, Dublin would have 499 pubs, instead of its 1,551; Belfast would have 416 instead of 1,110, Waterford could suffice with 44 pubs instead of 232, and in Clonmel 18 would be adequate, but where, in fact, there were 113.

In its comments on this unhealthy state of affairs the Commission reported that while the laws relating to the granting of licences had serious defects, the justices had misused those clear powers which they possessed and were solely responsible for a deplorable situation.

In their investigation into the administration of the law by the licensing authority, the Commissioners reported that in the five cities where the Recorder was the sole authority for granting public house licences these judges made valiant efforts to apply a defective law. But it was a very different situation in the smaller towns, where the administration of the licensing laws "was almost beyond belief.'

The most serious and most prevalent evil was the canvassing of justices and the packing of benches in order to obtain liquor licences. Not only were the justices approached for favours before licensing sessions, but even before prosecutions.

District Inspector F.J. Ball, of the Royal Irish Constabulary, Tralee, Co. Kerry, told the Commission of the extraordinary scenes he had witnessed at the quarter sessions in Midleton, Co. Cork:

"There was the largest attendance of magistrates I ever saw at Midleton. There was not room for them on the bench seats, they were standing closely packed on the steps of the bench, they were standing in the passages, and there was at least one down in the body of the court, apparently taking no part in the proceedings. The magistrates took evidence in a lot of cases and retired to consult.

"When they were retiring, a relative of one of the applicants rushed over to the magistrate who was in the body of the court and apparently not acting with the rest, and in my hearing said to him: 'Are you not a magistrate? Go in and vote.' He got the magistrate by the shoulders and pushed him on before him along the passage until, with a final heave, he thrust him among the magistrates who were retiring, and this magistrate went in with the others. That particular licence was granted."

District Inspector Ball said he knew of occasional, or special event, licences being granted without the consent of the publican in whose name they had been applied for, and he had known of bogus consents signed by fictitious or unqualified magistrates. One occasional licence was granted for a total abstinence fete.

Judge Orr said that in his Co. Down jurisdiction there were 302 justices. In one instance he presided over a court of 74 justices, sitting all over the courthouse. To work with such a number, he said, was quite impossible, especially as these magistrates in many cases refused to accept the ruling of the County Court Judge, even on points of law.

Rev. M. Ahern, curate of Ladysbridge, Catlemartyr, Co. Cork, said licences were granted in spite of objections by the clergy and the police, and without any evidence on behalf of the applicant.

He told how he was called upon in one instance by a canvasser, a relative of his own, and asked to use his influence with justices to get a particular licence granted.

80

William Jameson & Co's Distillery, Marrowbone Lane Dublin, 1878.

The man represented himself as being authorised by a Cork brewery to give five pounds, by way of expenses, to any magistrate who would attend and vote for the licence being granted.

The police had a frustrating time in their efforts to stamp out licensing abuses. District Inspector Ball referred to the case of a publican, with a six-day licence, who had been prosecuted by a constable for selling on a Sunday. It was a clear case, and three men were found drinking on the premises.

Three days before the hearing of the case two magistrates attended at the District Inspector's office and held an inquiry. They sent for the constable who had brought the charges, but neither the publican nor the three customers "found on" were present. The constable was not sworn but was called upon to state his complaint. Finally one of the magistrates said he would fine the publican £1. The second magistrate disagreed and said he would dismiss the charge.

On the court day, the following Monday, the case was entered for hearing, and when it was called the same two magistrates were the only ones present. They marked the case as dismissed without prejudice, without a single witness being called or examined.

The District Inspector told the Commission that this was but one of numerous such cases within his own knowledge.

Chapter 13

Spirit of the Scots

 WHY DID SCOTCH sweep ahead of Irish whiskey to win favour in the world markets, especially when Irish was the undisputed leader in the export trade?

The simple one-word answer is—blending. Despite its dubious beginnings, mixing, as it simply was in the early stages before blending whiskies became a skilled art, was the start of a transformation in the whiskey business. An additional explanation might be attributed to the apparent lack of perception and business acumen by the major Irish distilling companies who either failed to recognise, or disregarded, the signs of change.

To the pot still traditionalists, both manufacturers and consumers, any interference with the time-honoured methods of production, particularly the concept of mixing immature spirit with the real thing, was a heresy which would bring its own misfortune on the perpetrators. This view was soundly endorsed by the Irish home consumers who rejected the new whiskey as an inferior substitute.

In the early 1900s Irish was the sovereign whiskey, renowned in all countries where whiskey was drunk. More Irish pot still was exported than any other whiskey. But the Irish distilling companies complacently dismissed the indications that trends and tastes were shifting. The lighter blended whiskies were winning new markets everywhere and were gradually displacing the traditional malts. While the Scottish blenders were enjoying increasing success the Irish distilling companies remained stubbornly unimpressed. The new craze would not last, they insisted, there was no need to change their time-tested methods. It was a misjudgement for which the industry was to pay dearly.

The distillers were not alone in failing to recognise the moment of opportunity. With the outbreak of World War II and the severe shortages which followed, the Irish government decided to restrict still further the export of whiskey in order to preserve supplies for the home market—and so maintain the revenue from taxes.

The Scottish distilleries and blending houses, on the other hand, cut down wartime home supplies in order to build up exports and so win much-needed dollars for the British Government. And so wherever American troops were stationed in Europe the Scotch was there. And they continued to drink it when they returned home.

In 1877, just a year before *Truths About Whiskey* was published by Messrs John Jameson & Sons, William Jameson & Co., John Power and Son, and George Roe & Co., six of the oldest established Scottish grain whisky manufacturers came together to form the Distillers Company Ltd. This grouping marked the establishment of a solid foundation for the disciplined control and growth of the Scotch blended whiskey industry. It was also the beginning of what was to become one of the biggest trade organisations in Britain.

DCL owns 50 distilleries and about 75 brands with more than fifty per cent of the whisky export market.

One of the great names associated with DCL is that of William J. Ross, a farmer's son who joined the company as a clerk, rose to become managing director and, in 1925, chairman. Ross's dynamic leadership opened up sales outlets around the world and charted the company's expansion into diversified fields. It was Ross who put the final stamp of success on the company by ultimately bringing in the top names in the trade. The Dewars, the Haigs, the Walkers and the Buchanans joined up during the early 1920s, followed later by Mackie's White Horse Distilleries and Sanderson's (Vat 69). Bells and Teachers are two of the bigger firms who have remained outside the conglomerate. Teachers is now owned by Allied Breweries.

The entry of the famous 'whisky barons' opened up new horizons for the Distillers Company. When America ended its fourteen years of prohibition in December, 1933, the company was fully geared for a massive sales campaign. Their efforts were hampered by the industrial depression of the times, and it was not until the post-war years that Scotch whisky exports began to assume immense proportions.

The finely blended whiskies appealed to the American palate. Blending skills had now reached the degree of perfection. Each of the well-known brands had its own secrets, and as many as forty single whiskies could be utilised in the making of any one of the famous blends known today throughout the world.

The remarkable entrepreneurs, the dynamic salesmen who made Scotch the most popular international drink in the twentieth century were mostly second generation, sons of the founders who had begun in humble circumstances. Perhaps the most renowned of these was Tommy Dewar.

In the 1860s Thomas Robert Dewar, then 21, joined his elder brother, John Alexander, in the Perth wine merchant's establishment founded by their father, who had started as an apprentice. The younger son was sent to London to sell Dewar's whisky. And sell it he did. Tommy was a born salesman, witty, dapper and full of energy and ideas. Having conquered London he embarked on overseas tours and returned with full order books. Both brothers were eventually raised to the peerage.

Lord Dewar, still 'Tommy' to his friends and business acquaintances, was a patron and benefactor of sport, notably racing and football, and of course renowned for his witticisms, 'Do right and fear no man. Don't write and fear no woman,' 'Golf is not necessarily a rich man's game, there are some very poor players.' Lord Tommy Dewar died a bachelor in 1930, and despite his jovial personality he remained an abstemious man.

John Walker, a farmer's son, opened a small grocery business in Kilmarnock in the year 1820. He subsequently brought in his son, Alexander, who later changed the business into a wholesale firm and started bottling whisky. He opened a London branch and pioneered export sales of 'Johnnie Walker' which eventually became the largest selling Scotch in the world, and its maker became Sir Alexander Walker.

Sir Peter Mackie, who created White Horse whisky, was the nephew of a Glasgow distiller. The whisky was named after an historic Edinburgh inn. Mackie was a man of striking physique, forceful personality and restless energy. In 1924 the firm of Mackie and Co. was dissolved and reconstituted as White Horse Distillers Ltd.

James Buchanan was working for a whisky company in London when, at the age of 35, he borrowed money to set up his own company. He marketed a new brand which he labelled as Buchanan's Blend, but his customers insisted on calling it Black and White, because of the stark white label on the black bottle, and eventually the label was changed to incorporate the famous pair of black and white dogs. Buchanan was raised to the peerage as Lord Woolavington. He was a flamboyant personality who enjoyed life to the full. His racehorses won the Epsom Derby and the St. Leger. He was also a generous benefactor of medical and educational institutions. He died in 1935 at the age of 85.

So, helped along by vigorous marketing and promotion, Scotch blended whisky gradually won for itself a strong position in world markets, particularly America. It made millionaires and peers of its top trade leaders and is today a basic pillar in Britain's economic structure. One can only reflect that all this achievement was made possible by the invention of an Irish excise official, an invention that was first offered to the leading Irish distillers, but rejected by them. The Highlands malt whiskies too are in a healthy state. As well as supplying the grain distilleries with malt for blending they enjoy a good home and export trade as prestige whiskies.

By contrast Irish whiskey had lost out badly in the export business as the pot still versus blended controversy rumbled indecisively on. Some of the smaller Irish distillers were keen on getting into the blended business but the Dublin companies still maintained their conservative attitude about interfering with their traditional and high quality products.

In 1926 the compulsory bonding period for Irish whiskey was raised from three to five years. The ostensible purpose was to make an even finer whiskey but it also served to protect the trade against imports of Scotch. Imported whiskey had to be sold at the legal age laid down in the country of origin. The grain whisky used in the imported Scotch was unlikely to be more than three years old. But similarly, Irish had now to be kept for five years before it could be sold in America, thus creating another export barrier. It was not until 1969 that the restricted period was reduced to the conventional three-year term, at the request of the distillers.

Whiskey in the wood, on its slow journey to maturity.

Chapter 14

Division in the Dáil

 DEBATES IN DÁIL Eireann on the Irish whiskey industry reflected the division of opinion that had inhibited the trade's forward expansion.

In June, 1953, the Minister for Industry and Commerce, Sean Lemass, summarised his own view of the whiskey situation. He was replying to Deputy Jack McQuillan, who introduced a motion urging the government to give special assistance to whiskey exports. Mr. McQuillan noted that the value of Irish whiskey exports in 1952 amounted to just under £500,000. Exports of Scotch for the same period represented £32.5 million.

Mr. Lemass said the government had imposed restrictions on exports of whiskey during the wartime emergency period. This was done in order to conserve home supplies as far as possible and to maintan excise revenue. He agreed that this was in contrast to the policy of the British government, who facilitated dollar exports of Scotch whisky and left the home market short.

Mr. Lemass went on to say that the predominance of Scotch in the world export markets had begun fifty years earlier, and no matter who was responsible for the mistaken commercial policy followed by the Irish distillers then, there was nothing they could do about it now. He said it was his view that the world market was for a Scotch type of whiskey, but not all Irish distillers agreed with this view. The distillers considered that they had built up a fair export trade in pot still whiskey and they might well jeopardise that trade by marketing as Irish whiskey a blended product of the Scotch type.

Mr. James Dillon, an opposition spokesman noted for his sometimes fearsome eloquence, disagreed totally with the Lemass view. If the government was instrumental in bringing pressure to bear on the pot still distillers to produce a synthetic product for the foreign market against their better judgement, he believed they were acting most recklessly and imprudently. Irish whiskey is pot still whiskey, Scotch is blended whisky, a blend of pot still and patent still and if anyone was nursing the illusion that he could break into the American market with a 'Scotch' whisky distilled in Ireland, then he was just crazy, Mr. Dillon declared.

In 1952 the Fianna Fáil government dealt the drink trade a shattering blow by raising the excise duty on home-produced spirits by £1.19s per proof gallon, causing a price rise of 6d per glass, a serious imposition indeed in those depressed times. In the budget debate that followed, the government was accused of injuring an important native industry, already suffering decline. Finance Minister Seán MacEntee's assurance that the duty on Irish spirit was probably the lowest in the world, and the retail selling price likewise, 3s 6d a glass against 5s a glass in Northern Ireland, apparently did not impress the voters, who ousted Fianna Fáil in the following general election which brought in a Fine Gael-Labour coalition.

In November 1954 Deputy McQuillan, an Independent, again raised the matter when, in private member's business, he introduced a measure proposing that in view of the failure to secure adequate markets abroad for Irish whiskey under existing production conditions, steps should be taken to promote exports, if necessary by setting up a state-sponsored company to produce a suitably blended Irish whiskey.

Jack McQuillan recalled the past glories of Irish whiskey, with some historical detail and criticised the complacent attitude of the distillers and urged them to come together and build a new distillery for the production of blended whiskey. A prosperous distilling industry was essential to the national economy, ensuring excellent employment for workers, a rich cash crop for the farmer, barley for the maltsters and whiskey for export.

Seán Lemass, now in the opposition benches, referred to Mr. McQuillan's interesting account of the efforts made fifty years earlier by the Irish distillers to secure the recommendation of a British Royal Commission for the making of a law which would prohibit the use of the word 'whiskey' except in association with the pot still product. They were right to try it, declared Mr. Lemass, adding that the great majority of drinkers in Ireland would hold the view that the only drink worthy of being called whiskey was pot still whiskey.

He could well understand the reluctance of the main Irish distillers who for many years had been producing good pot still whiskey to turn now to the production of an inferior blended product. But they had to recognise that the bulk of the export markets of the world was interested mainly in the lighter blends, which sold chiefly as Scotch.

Mr. Lemass's successor as Industry and Commerce Minister, Mr. William Norton, outlined the efforts made by the existing and previous governments at improving whiskey exports. There were several discussions with the distillers on the subject of exports. The distillers were reluctant to expand production in the absence of a guaranteed market, and preferred to keep to the traditional pattern of business, he told the Dáil.

He said that in June 1953 Coras Trachtala, the Irish Export Board, was directed to initiate a scheme with the distillers with a view towards developing overseas markets for blended Irish whiskey. A preliminary survey in America showed that while the distribution of Irish whiskey was satisfactory, it did not sell sufficiently well because of the lack of publicity. Fifty per cent of the whiskey drinkers questioned in the United States at the time said they had never heard of Irish whiskey!

Mr. Norton said he was satisfied that there was a market in America for blended Irish whiskey as well as traditional pot still, and the matter would have tò be strongly pursued.

The Irish distilling industry has had to bear many burdens, mostly inflicted at the whim of successive governments in the form of penal taxation which made survival difficult enough and effectively discouraged plans for expansion. Nevertheless in recent years progressive new thinking and radical policy changes by a more enlightened generation of industrial leaders have at last swept away the inhibiting barriers of prejudice and revitalised the industry.

The changes may have been difficult, but they were

necessary in order to guide the industry to a position whereby its superb products would attain their deserved recognition and favour in world markets.

Dáil Eireann, Dublin.

Chapter 15

The Irish Outlook

 A SAGACIOUS observer of the international whiskey trade once summarised the business with this comment: the Irish can make it, the Scots can sell it, and the Americans can drink it.

Now the Irish are really beginning to sell it—to the rest of the world, that is. Yes of course you could always buy Irish whiskey in San Francisco or West Berlin, but you had to be lucky, lucky enough to get a bartender who would search diligently behind the rows of Scotch to find, eventually, a bottle of Powers Gold Label or John Jameson. Not so long ago if you asked for Irish in a Brooklyn bar you would most likely come face to face with a bottle bearing a shamrock-spattered label proclaiming the contents to be something called Pride of Erin, or worse. Thankfully these dubious concoctions have been swept from the shelves and only the long-established Irish-made brands are available.

The Irish whiskey export industry is now soundly based and pushing ahead, with the main concentration on the U.S. market. Specially selected distributors of impeccable repute have been appointed in key centres and the multi-million dollar marketing, promotional and advertising programmes have been keyed to the well-known brands, each with its distinctive characteristics, but all presenting an image of quality and prestige.

Nevertheless the task of breaking into the conservative liquor market requires courage and faith of a high order, especially when the market is dominated by the native Bourbons and Ryes and the popular Scotches. For the Irish exporters it is made more difficult in having to overcome the mistakes and misjudgements of the past and creating a whole new concept of Irish whiskey.

The Irish distillers of the 19th century were zealously

Reputed to be Ireland's oldest Pub. The Brazen Head
in Bridgefoot Street, Dublin.

proud of the quality of their products, and none can reproach them for their upright attitude. Irish pot still was, and is, foremost among the world's great whiskies. But looking back today, a hundred years later, it is easy to question their judgement and business sense, their failure to read the signs and recognise the trends. Even when the Scots swept into the old traditional markets with their lighter blends the Irish refused to compromise. As far as they were concerned the rest of the world was out of step. The fact that new grain distilleries were rising quickly in Scotland also failed to impress them. And today one naturally feels that those great Irish whiskey houses could have capitalised on Aeneas Coffey's revolutionary new patent still for export purposes without fear of endangering their reputation either at home or abroad.

But whatever about the reasoning behind the board-room decisions, the opportunity was lost. Trickles of Irish whiskey to overseas countries continued, but only in the last ten years or so have the rigid attitudes of the past been finally buried and a serious and determined drive made to win a rightful share of the world whiskey trade. The preference for a lighter-textured whiskey, suitable for drinking American-style, on the rocks, or even neat, is now universal, although many people like to make their whiskey a pleasantly innocuous long drink with liberal helpings of 'mixers.' The challenging task for the new breed of Irish distillers was to produce a whiskey which would conform with today's taste requirements and still preserve its uniquely Irish character.

Irish pot still continues to be a highly favoured drink, but there is not so much of it around nowadays. The appellation has gradually disappeared from the labels of both the home and export products over the last few years. Now only the special Jameson 15-year-old remains to satisfy the discriminating demands of the traditionalists.

It required intensive study and research and all the skills of the blending experts to achieve a result so subtle and successful that the gradual changeover from pure pot still to blended was scarcely noticed in the home market. Of course one very good reason for this is that pot still spirit remains the premier ingredient of the various blends.

94

The column still in the former Powers Distillery in John's Lane, Dublin.

The launching of the new Irish blends in the United States, handsomely packaged and presented, was encouragingly successful. Indeed by 1980 approximately 50 per cent of all Irish whiskey production was being exported.

To get a clear picture of Irish progress in the United State we can turn to the statistics and comments as set out in *Liquor Handbook*, that formidable American publication regarded as the bible of the industry. Quote:

'Sales of Irish whiskey again increased impressively during the 1978 calendar year. Editors of the Handbook estimate the year's total at 247,348 cases, a 17.8 percent gain over the 209,969 cases of 1977. Except for rum, this was the largest percentage gain among the categories.

'Irish whiskey sales are growing around the world, in addition to their continued impact in the United States. It is estimated that world-wide sales of the product have grown at a compound annual rate of 19 percent in the past ten years, and that they will increase by an annual compound rate of 16.1 percent for the next ten.

'The coveted million-case year for Irish whiskey in the United States is still some years in the future but does now seem a certain eventuality.'

The meticulous and varied analyses relating to the sales of Irish (and all other whiskies) in the Handbook, such as the month by month, state by state returns, brings forth the editorial observation that the image of Irish has changed from being merely a St. Patrick's Day ritual to a much more exemplary identity, and notes that the very high portion of annual demand manifested in December shows clearly that Irish whiskey is prized as a gift item and that its distinctive character is now being recognised and appreciated by the American general public. All the Irish brands are in the higher priced prestige classifications.

These are encouraging signs, but they are still only a beginning. The Irish share of the U.S. market is still around the lowly one per cent mark, or about the same amount of imported American whiskey sales in Ireland. Nevertheless the initial impact of the new quality Irish campaign has been quite impressive, and all the indications and projections suggest that in the years ahead Irish whiskey will achieve increasing consumer acceptance, not only in the United States but also in

Midleton, showing the copper pot stills scaled to traditional shape.

Canada and the EEC countries, of which West Germany is its best customer.

Frank O'Reilly, head of the John Power company, was the chief architect behind the 1966 consensus of the major Dublin and Cork distilling firms to amalgamate. He impressed the individual companies that only a marketing merger could bring about the necessary strength and unity of purpose to compete successfully in the international spirit markets.

O'Reilly was elected chairman of the new grouping, initially called United Distillers of Ireland Ltd. He brought in Kevin McCourt, one of Ireland's foremost business executives, as managing director, with a mandate to shape up the company for a determined new export initiative. McCourt, in turn, recruited, in 1969, Archie Cook, a Scot of proven marketing ability, and these two spearheaded the new impulse. When Kevin McCourt announced his active retirement in 1978 Irish Distillers had moved ahead on all fronts and secured a sound foothold in the paramount American market. He was succeeded as managing director by Richard Burrows, a dynamic young executive who had been closely associated with the remarkable upsurge of Old Bushmills whiskey in the 1970s.

The decision to build a new distillery, the first in Ireland for more than a hundred years, was inevitable. The great Dublin houses of Jameson and Power at Bow Street and John's Lane, in the heart of the old city, were now hemmed in with no possibility of further physical expansion. It was a hard decision to phase out these renowned Dublin landmarks which had given nearly two centuries of service and generations of highly valued employment.

But it had to be. The old era was dying and the new horizons emerging. As Dublin's long distilling tradition passed quietly into history Midleton arose, the symbol of a revitalised Irish industry, the world's most modern distillery. The new Co. Cork complex was completed in July 1975, and as it steamed into productive action its venerable neighbour, Old Midleton, slowed to a nostalgic halt.

Dublin's link with the distilling industry will be retained with the splendid new head office building at Smithfield, erected on the site of the old John Jameson spirits store, adjoining Bow Street.

The magnificent natural environment of the Midleton location is perfect for the distilling process. Situated in the heart of the barley country, with ample supplies of pure clear water, it also affords acres of room for future expansion. The large modern complex has an annual production capacity of seven million proof gallons of whiskey and neutral spirit for making gin and vodka. There are four steam-heated copper pot stills, each of 17,000 gallons capacity, and five giant column stills. Numerous single-story warehouses each contain 1.2 million proof gallons of whiskey, maturing in oak casks.

The design of the plant incorporates a system of integrated facilities, and the new equipment represents the highest levels of modern distilling technology, allied of course to the indispensable traditional craft of hand and eye, and allowing for each of the well-known brands to be produced with its own unique characteristics.

It can be argued that Irish Distillers Group is a monopoly power, and it is true to say that IDG is now the sole supplier of genuine Irish whiskey throughout the world. But imported Scotch which accounts for an approximate 25 percent of the Irish home market, is a very formidable opposition, and in the general domestic spirits field vodka has climbed to an impressive 19 percent, while gin maintains a steady 10 percent share.

Unlike the Irish distillers of the past who were happy enough with the fruits of an assured domestic sales supremacy, their successors today have to live in a severely competitive world. A secure foothold in the United States market is a prize worth striving for. But it is not easy. Of all consumer groups, the market researchers will tell you, drinkers are the most conservative. They have to be cajoled and persuaded—not so much to change their drinking habits but merely to sample something that is new to them. To be successful, the "conversion" process has to rely on two main factors, an impressive and intensive publicity campaign, and a high quality product that justifies the claims made for it.

To launch an export marketing drive you need faith, courage and capital. You also need a buoyant home market as a base of operations. What you don't need is a harsh national budget to impede and frustrate the expansion movement.

The government budget of January, 1979 put another 6p on the glass of spirits, a penalty that made Irish the second highest taxed whiskey among the EEC countries, next to Denmark. In 1980 the government levied another 16p on the glass of whiskey, raising the retail home cost to about £1.25, approximately half of which (62p) was made up of government excise duty and value added tax.

Exports of Scotch whisky earn more than £500 million annually for Britain. If Irish whiskey exports rose by even 2 percent this would have a significantly beneficial effect on the Irish economy.

Distilling is a traditional national industry, rooted in the very soil of Ireland. *Uisce beatha*, liquid essence of the barley, is an agricultural product, processed and perfected by modern technology and native craft. The industry gives satisfying employment for more than a thousand workers in a variety of grades and occupations. Irish whiskey is a high quality product which deserves to be known and enjoyed throughout the world.

Chapter 16

Whiskey across the World

ON THIS SIDE of the world we may tend to overlook the great American whiskey tradition. The United States is the world's foremost whiskey producer, as well as being the biggest market, the land of hope and glory for every whiskey company in other countries. America imports much more whiskey than she exports but the native bourbons and ryes are still the American favourites, selling more than twice as much as imported Scotch and Canadian.

Whiskey making in the U.S. goes back to the era of the pioneers who trekked westwards after the Revolutionary War of 1175-77. President George Washington had affirmative views on the subject of whiskey. In 1777 he wrote to the Continental Congress: "I would beg leave to suggest the propriety of erecting ...distilleries in different states. The benefits arising from the moderate use of strong liquor ... are not to be disputed."

But, ironically, it was Washington's government that touched off America's historic whiskey rebellion by enforcing the first excise tax on distilled spirits.

Many of the early migrant farmers from the east, mostly Irish and Scottish settlers, moved into West Pennsylvania where they turned large stretches of wasteland into productive farms, with abundant crops of rye, oats, maize and wheat. The industrious pioneers converted their surplus grain into whiskey, for which they found a ready sale, and a thriving rye whiskey distilling industry arose. In 1791 fiscal problems forced the U.S. government to levy a tax of seven cents on every gallon of whiskey produced, plus 54 cents a gallon on the capacity of every still.

The pioneer distillers angrily refused to submit to this imposition and reacted violently. Excise officials dispatched to collect the toll were attacked, some of them tarred and feathered. The home of Sir John Neville, regional inspector of excise, was set on fire. Negotiations with the militant farmers were fruitless and the whiskey rebellion raged on until 1794, when President Washington ordered a force of 15,000 soldiers, led by Gen. Henry Lee, Governor of Virginia, to quell the mutiny. President Washington rode part of the way with the militiamen. The farmer-distillers were subdued after a brief confrontation.

Many of the early migrant farmers from the East, moved on rather than submit to the excise men. They found remote areas of Kentucky very favourable for their activities. From this beginning Kentucky eventually became the foremost whiskey-producing state, and the home of Bourbon, named after the local Bourbon county.

Bourbon is made from malted wheat or barley on a mash of maize, or corn as it is called in America. Its Pennsylvania rival uses rye as the basic cereal, with malted rye or barley. Canadian whiskies are made much in the U.S. manner but are somewhat lighter bodied than the American ryes and bourbons. Most American whiskey is blended but there remains a strong market for 'straight', or matured pot still whiskey.

Whiskey, of sorts, is now made in several countries. There have been many jokes about 'Japanese Scotch' in the past, like the label proclaiming that the whiskey was made 'from genuine Scotch grapes.' Another brand was allegedly named 'King Anne Scotch.' But the whiskey people in Scotland and Ireland—and America—are not laughing any more, Oriental whiskey has now mastered the western production techniques and is becoming a serious export challenger. Leading the Japanese distilling upsurge is the giant Suntory company, which claims to have the world's largest distillery at Hakushu, in an Alpine setting. The Japanese import bulk malt from many countries, including Scotland, from where she also buys peat to help in producing 'Scotch-style' blends. Japan also sells bulk whiskey to bottlers in Brazil, Mexico, Philippines, Thailand and other countries. Eastern Europe is now served by Bulgarian bottlers of Japanese whiskey. South Korea has also gone into the spirit trade. A large modern distillery in Seoul was

The traditional method of spreading the malting barley on the malthouse floor.

completed in 1978 and offered attractive salaries to blenders and processing engineers experienced in the production of Scotch whisky.

One of the lovely old engraved mirrors issued to publicans by the Dublin Distillers.

Chapter 17

Proof of the Matter

YOU CAN NOW buy Irish whiskey in Moscow and Tokyo as well as in 100 or so other capital cities of the world. The business of shipping it into foreign markets is a complex operation that requires specialised knowledge and skills, and it often calls for ingenuity and patience.

The importation of distilled spirits, more than almost any other commodity, is enmeshed in a tangle of laws and regulations that vary from country to country. Irish Distillers have to use about 500 different export labels, each setting forth mandatory information regarding the contents of each container. More than forty bottle shapes and sizes are required in order to conform with various national regulations. Scores of documents may be necessary for a single shipment to meet legal and administrative conditions. Many countries also enforce formidable import duties in order to discourage too much competition with the national products.

Intricacies arise from the fact that three different systems of assessing alcoholic strength are in use in different parts of the world. In North America the United States proof measure is applied; in most continental European countries the Guy Lussac system is used, and in Britain and Commonwealth countries, as in Ireland, the Sykes method prevails. Proof strength determines the amount of duty imposed. Proof spirit is reckoned as being "100 percent proof."

The definition by the Irish Revenue Commissioners states: "The duty on spirits, whether imported or home produced, is charged by reference to the 'proof' strength. Proof spirit means such spirit as at the temperature of 51 degrees Fahrenheit weighs twelve thirteenths of an equal measure of distilled water at the same temperature."

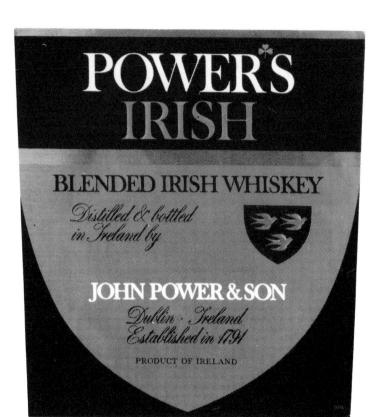

POWER'S IRISH

BLENDED IRISH WHISKEY

Distilled & bottled in Ireland by

JOHN POWER & SON

Dublin · Ireland
Established in 1791

PRODUCT OF IRELAND

★ ★ ★

OLD BUSHMILLS

IRISH WHISKEY

Blended & Bottled by
The Old Bushmills Distillery Co.
LIMITED

BUSHMILLS
COUNTY ANTRIM

PRODUCT OF IRELAND
70.31 ML   2.47 FL OZ
40% alc/vol   70 PROOF
REGISTERED LABEL

JAMESON

IRISH WHISKEY

70 Pf PRODUCT OF IRELAND

Tullamore Dew

BLENDED IRISH WHISKEY

RECETA PARA IRISH COFFEE

1. Echar en una copa precalentada una medida de TULLAMORE DEW Irish Whiskey — este Whiskey que combina tan naturalmente con café.

2. Rellenar la copa hasta 1½ centímetros del borde con un café ardiente muy caliente y fuerte.

3. Añadir azúcar al gusto y mezclar bien.

4. Acabar por una capa de nata ligeramente batida.

N.B. Después de añadir la nata no hay que remover más, porque se obtiene el sabor único del Tullamore DEW al café caliente y el Irish Whiskey a través de la nata fría fresca.

A LIQUEUR OF DISTINCTION

THREE SWALLOW

In simple terms proof spirits contain approximately equal weights of alcohol and water.

Spirits in Ireland and Britain are generally sold at a strength of 30 degrees under proof, or 70 percent of proof strength, which means in effect about 40 percent pure alcohol and 60 percent water. The American definition of proof strength means that the Irish and British standard of 70 proof is equivalent to 80 proof in the United States. The hydrometer used to measure spirit strength was introduced by one Bartholomew Sykes in England in 1818 and is still in use today.

American measures are marginally higher than those in Britain and Ireland. The customary bottle of Irish or Scotch contains 26 2/3 fluid ounces, or one and one-third pints. The U.S. fluid ounce is slightly higher than the British and Irish equivalent.

But over-the-counter measures are more generous in Ireland than elsewhere. The standard Irish spirits measure is 2½ fluid ounces to the glass, or four 'half-ones' to the gill, which is five fluid ounces, or one quarter of a pint. The customary English measure is six drinks to the gill.

In former years Irish whiskey was traditionally stronger than the popular Scotch blends, but the Licensing Act of 1960, among other reforms, allowed Irish to be diluted from its customary 75 degrees proof strength to 70 proof, bringing it into line with the Scotch brands.

The legal definition of the Irish product was enacted by Dáil Eireann in the Irish Whiskey Act 1960 which laid down that in order to qualify for the title of Irish Whiskey the spirit must be distilled in the State from a mash of malt and cereal grains. Similarly the term Irish Pot Still Whiskey requires that the spirit be distilled in the State solely in pot stills from a mash of cereal grains normally grown in the State.

Whiskey matures only in the wood, oaken casks which allow it to 'breathe,' once bottled it ceases to age any further. The mystery of maturation remains one of nature's secrets. It has been lightly suggested that the discovery of whiskey mellowing with age was made by the early roving distillers who were forced to conceal their precious product from the excise eyes by burying it in casks and leaving it undisturbed for long periods, whereupon on being disinterred and sampled it was found that the flavour and quality of the whiskey had wondrously improved.

The only distillation and bottling of potable spirits now carried on in Dublin continues in the Naas Road premises of Gilbey's of Ireland Ltd., where they produce their well-known gin and Smirnoff Vodka. The great wine and spirits firm of W. & A. Gilbey Ltd. started as a family business in England in 1857, and within a few years a branch was established in Dublin. Gilbey's bought large quantities of whiskey in bulk from John Jameson and Sons, holding the casks in storage in their own bonded warehouses in Dublin. From this arrangement came the famous Gilbey brand of Redbreast twelve year-old whiskey, still as popular as ever.

Alec Waugh in his book, "Merchants of Wine," (1957), a centenary record of the House of Gilbey, says that Gilbeys held a larger stock of Irish whiskey than any other firm in the world, and recalls that in the year 1875 Gilbey's sold 83,000 dozen Irish to 38,000 Scotch. A bottle of good whiskey at that time cost 3s 6d.

Two other old-established Dublin wine and spirit merchants still market their own brand of Irish whiskey, Millar's Black Label and Mitchell's Green Spot.

Gilbeys of Ireland use a 500-gallon copper pot still for their gin and vodka processes. In gin manufacturing the grain spirit is re-distilled to remove all impurities and then undergoes a third distillation in the pot still, with juniper berries and other botanical flavouring agents, such as coriander seed, added. Gin does not require maturing. The name is derived from *geneva*, the Dutch word for juniper.

In vodka distillation all flavouring elements are removed by a process of charcoal filtration, leaving only the pure spirit. Vodka is generally sold in western countries at a strength of 65.5 degrees proof.

Gilbeys of Ireland also had the distinction of creating and marketing a successful new drink product in recent years. Baileys Original Irish Cream, a liqueur using Irish whiskey and Irish cream, was quietly launched in 1974 and within a few short years had attained an impressive export performance, a success story that encouraged imitators in some countries.

Chapter 18

Famous Irish Distilleries

 WHISKEY MAKING in one form or another is probably as old as the hills of Ireland, we shall never know just when or where it began. The origins of the licensed distillery industry are almost as vague, the few references we have seem to agree only that it began in Dublin around the mid 18th century. A *History of Dublin* published in the year 1818 compiled by Warburton, Whitelaw and Walsh, says whiskey was introduced to the city in 1750, to challenge the market for imported rum and brandy. It records that in the year 1816 two million gallons of whiskey were distilled in Dublin. 6,000 gallons were exported to London, 4,000 gallons to New York, 40 gallons to Quebec and—wait for it—60,000 gallons to Lisbon. The Portuguese importers, it explains, favoured Irish whiskey as a fortifying agent for Port wine!

Old Bushmills Distillery

The two main productive distilleries now under the control of Irish Distilleries Group Ltd., New Midleton in the south and Old Bushmills in the north, are certainly unique in the fact that one is the world's newest distillery (at the time of writing) and the other is the world's oldest.

It is on record that in the year 1608 Sir Thomas Phillips, who represented King James I in Ulster, officially instituted the Bushmills distillery in Co. Antrim. Historical references to distillation in the Bushmills locality can in fact be traced back to the year 1494.

When Alfred Barnard visited the pleasant village of Bushmills about 1886 he described in vivid fashion the

Old Bushmills, one of the oldest distilleries in the world was 'instituted' in 1608.

six-mile trip from Portrush by the electric railway 'climbing hills and high rocks overhanging the sea, and crossing the Bush, a fine salmon river.' He found the compact distillery very much up to date and 'a model of brightness and cleanliness.'

The water used in the making of Old Bushmills whiskey comes from the same soure today as it did when the distillery was first started. This is St. Columb's Rill, a tributary of the River Bush which flows past the distillery. The water used for the distillation rises in peaty ground and flows over basalt rock. Old Bushmills is distinctive from most other whiskies in that it is a unique blend of one malt and one grain whiskey.

The distillery's ownership changed frequently. In the 1880s it became the Old Bushmills Distillery Co. Ltd., with Samuel W. Boyd as its head. It remained with the Boyd family until the late 1940s. In 1964 it was acquired by Bass Charrington, and it was subsequently purchased by Seagram, the giant Canadian group. By arrangement with Seagram, Irish Distillers obtained a controlling interest in the company, and in January 1978, Seagram disposed of its remaining 20 percent holding to Irish Distillers.

In recent years the distillery has been expanded to twice its original size, new warehouses have been added and output greatly increased. Bushmills has a long-standing reputation for its high quality and fine flavour, and the renowned Black Bush liqueur whiskey is a drink relished by connoisseurs.

John Jameson and Son Ltd
Bow St. Distillery

The father figure of the Irish distilling trade is surely John Jameson. 'Old John,' as he came to be affectionately known, was a shrewd Scot who arrived in Dublin in the 1770s and subsequently founded one of the world's great whiskey houses. The famous Bow Street distillery was already established in a small way when he bought himself a share in the business. By the year 1800 he had acquired full control and introduced his two sons to the business. John was well connected in the whiskey trade. His wife was a member of the Haig family, one of the oldest and most illustrious of the Scotch whisky

Powers Distillery at the turn of the century, this building in Thomas Street
Dublin, was known as the Counting House.

houses, one of whose chairmen was Douglas Earl Haig, Commander-in-Chief of the British forces in France during World War I.

J. J.'s eldest son, also John, became owner of the Bow Street distillery, and the second son, William, ran the Marrowbone Lane distillery, previously owned by John Stein, a member of a well-known Scottish distilling family. Another Jameson brother was associated with a distillery near Enniscorthy, Co. Wexford, whose daughter married Guiseppe Marconi, and their son was the inventor of wireless telegraphy.

Old John was a stern and resolute man of high ideals. He impressed his employees that they would be well paid, with the best possible working conditions. In return for all these benefits their task would be to produce the finest whiskey in the world.

The Bow Street distillery grew in size and stature, eventually covering several acres of ground. John Jameson employed the highest skills in distillation, used the best equipment available and bought only the finest materials, paying the highest prices for the best Irish barley. He invested immense capital in laying down great quantities of whiskey in sherry casks, to repose for many years in the dark vaults, so necessary in order to achieve that body and flavour which, John insisted, must excel all others.

The bonded warehouses of the Jameson distillery, long cloister-like avenues stacked with casks of ageing whiskey, ran deep under the city of Dublin. At any given time more than two million gallons of whiskey were slowly maturing.

Production at the Bow Street distillery ceased in 1971, and was transferred to the John Power distillery at John's Lane pending the ultimate move to the new Midleton complex in Co. Cork. Members of the Jameson family have been associated with the company in an unbroken line for the past 200 years.

John Power & Son Ltd.
John's Lane Distillery

The last of the great whiskey houses to cease operations in Dublin was John Power and Son, in John's

Lane, established in 1791. Although the renowned Power's Gold Label brand continues to be produced in Midleton in still greater quantities, and with all the meticulous care that has made it the top-selling whiskey in Ireland, the dismantling in 1976 of the famous distillery regretfully signalled the end of a centuries-old Dublin tradition.

The distillery was set up by James Power, but it was his son and successor, John, a man of infinite energy and ability, who extended and eventually rebuilt the premises, covering over six acres, and incorporating the most up-to-date equipment. The workforce of nearly 300 enjoyed excellent conditions of employment.

The site of the original distillery was occupied by a hostelry, owned by James Power, from which the mail coaches departed for the north and west of Ireland.

Sir John. Power, as he became, initiated many developments in the industry. The company pioneered the use of miniature bottles—the famous 'Baby Power'—for which special Government legislation had to be passed. The distillery was also the first to bottle its own whiskey, the common practice then being to sell the produce in bulk to wholesalers and retailers. The first steam engine erected in Ireland was installed in the distillery, as also was the first dynamo to supply electric current in Dublin.

Sir John Power was made High Sheriff of Dublin, and on September 23, 1854, he laid the foundation stone for the magnificent O'Connell Monument in Dublin. Frank O'Reilly, present Chairman of the John Power Company and Chairman of Irish Distillers Group Ltd., is a direct descendant of Sir John Power.

Alfred Barnard, to whose diligence we owe much of our information about Irish distilleries of the past, was highly impressed with his visit to the John's Lane distillery, the spacious layout, the machinery and equipment and the general air of efficiency. He regarded it as "far superior to many I have seen throughout the United Kingdom, as complete a work as is possible to find anywhere."

The Still House held five large pot stills "all kept as bright and keen as burnished gold." There were seventeen bonded warehouses within the complex and the company had additional bonded stores in the basement of the then new railway at Westland Row.

Barnard referred glowingly to the great engine rooms, the boiler house, the model stalls for the splendid shire horses, the harness room and the 'horse hospital' or special sick boxes, the coach house; all were well-equipped and maintained with meticulous care. The handsome building fronting Thomas Street led into spacious public and private offices, dining- and visitors' rooms.

At lunch in the distillery Barnard sampled some special old Powers which, he said, was finer than anything he had ever tasted. "Perfect in flavour and as pronounced in the ancient aroma of Irish whiskey, so dear to the hearts of connoisseurs, as one could possibly desire," he wrote.

George Roe & Co. Ltd. Thomas St. Distillery

The Thomas Street Distillery was established as a small unit by Peter Roe about 1757, and remained with the family all its life. It stood almost opposite the Guinness brewery, and is now part of the St. James's Gate complex. Coming under the ownership of George Roe and Co. Ltd., it was extended gradually to become the largest pot still distillery in the United Kingdom covering seventeen acres.

For a while the company achieved an annual output figure of two million gallons of whiskey with a large export trade to the United States, Britain and Canada. A smaller distillery in nearby Pimlico, run by another member of the family, Nicholas Roe, was taken over by the Thomas St. company

In 1889 the Dublin firms of George Roe & Co., William Jameson & Co. of Marrowbone Lane and the Dublin Whiskey Distillery in Jones's Road amalgamated to form a giant trading unit known as the Dublin Distilling Company Ltd., while preserving their own individual brands.

The main building of the George Roe plant was pleasantly distinctive with its ivy-covered walls and well-kept flower beds. A unique Dublin landmark, still standing is the 150-foot high windmill, which at one time supplied the motive power for the entire works. The mill

THE CELEBRATED

G R
WHISKEY.

Distillers' Guarantee of Purity
and Age.

SEVEN YEARS OLD.

Price **3/6** per Bottle.

In Cases of 2 Gallons (Carriage Paid), 42/-

Wholesale only:

THE DUBLIN DISTILLERS' CO.,
LIMITED,

(Geo. Roe & Co.), **DUBLIN**.

ESTABLISHED 1757.

If any difficulty is experienced in obtaining this **Whiskey** from your WINE MERCHANT or GROCER, please write direct to the Distillery for the name and address of the nearest Trader selling same. On receipt of application, with 8d. in stamps to cover cost of postage, a FREE SAMPLE will be forwarded.

Old Advertisement.

was surmounted by a large copper dome from which arose the dominant iron-cast figure of St. Patrick. And the patron saint, with mitre and crozier, still happily looks down on the much-changed scene of today. With the progression to steam power a 120-foot chimney stack was built behind the old mill. This was constructed by the company's own workmen in just under two years and was completed in 1868.

The company employed about 200 workers — engineers, fitters, coopers, blacksmiths, carpenters and painters. Eight pot stills were in use, from 12,000 to 20,000 gallon capacity. There were five steam engines and seven boilers.

George Roe's two sons, Henry and George, succeeded to the business in 1862 and added considerably to the company's progress. The wealthy Roe family contributed generously to cultural and charitable causes. In 1878 they handed over almost £250,000 for the restoration work on Dublin's 11th century Christ Church Cathedral.

Marrowbone Lane Distillery

The Marrowbone Lane Distillery (Dublin Distilling Co. Ltd.) was acquired by the Jameson family in 1799, with William Jameson as its head. It was then a small concern with an annual output of about 30,000 gallons of pot still whiskey. The new owners enlarged and re-equipped the plant at a cost of £300,000, creating employment for almost 200 workers, and boosting production to 200,000 gallons.

There were four pot stills of 9,000 to 18,000 gallon capacity, and nine bonded warehouses capable of storing 35,000 casks. Four steam engines and five boilers were in use. The cooperage department covered an acre of ground, employing eighty men in making, repairing, hooping and cleaning the casks. The main yard had fourteen stables, blacksmith shops, harness rooms, coach house and 'horse hospital,' and resembled a miniature cavalry barracks. The various buildings covered some fifteen acres.

The distillery was located close to the Grand Canal from which it drew its water supplies and its noted Dublin Whiskey was shipped to India, Australia, Canada and the West Indies among other markets.

Dublin Whiskey Distillery Co. Ltd.

The last wholly new distillery to be built in Dublin was that of the Dublin Whiskey Distillery Company, more familiarly known as D.W.D., at Jones Road, on the banks of the Tolka river.

Barnard tells us that the construction work began on July 22, 1872, and the distillery was in production exactly one year later. The building was finished in red brick, with a tall chimney stack rising imposingly from a courtyard just inside the main entrance. The distillery covered about seven acres and had a picturesque setting, partly surrounded by water and approached by a pleasantly rustic bridge.

A commercial and social review of Ireland published in 1892 by Stratten & Stratten of London assures us that the distillery was built on the site of the battlefield of Clontarf, where in 1014 King Brian Boru and his army routed the invading Danish marauders.

The first directors of the company were a group of Dublin businessmen who installed the latest equipment and engaged the best professional skills to manage the business. The seven original subscribers included W.G. Craig and R. Gardiner, directors of a well-known and still prominent Dublin accountancy firm.

The complex comprised a group of flat-roofed buildings. The 60-foot high still house, with four pot stills, had double tiers of wide iron galleries. The distillery plant was claimed to be practically fireproof. The flat roofs formed a system of reservoirs, one of which held 100,000 gallons of water. In addition, the supports of the various floors were hollow iron columns all filled with water. The main building was topped with an observatory which afforded panoramic views of the city and extending countryside. Much of the distillery's annual output of 560,000 gallons was exported to England and its colonies.

Phoenix Park Distillery

Among the Dublin whiskey companies of the late 19th century the Phoenix Park Distillery, formerly called the Chapelizod distillery, was unique in many respects. It was taken over and renamed by the Distillers Company

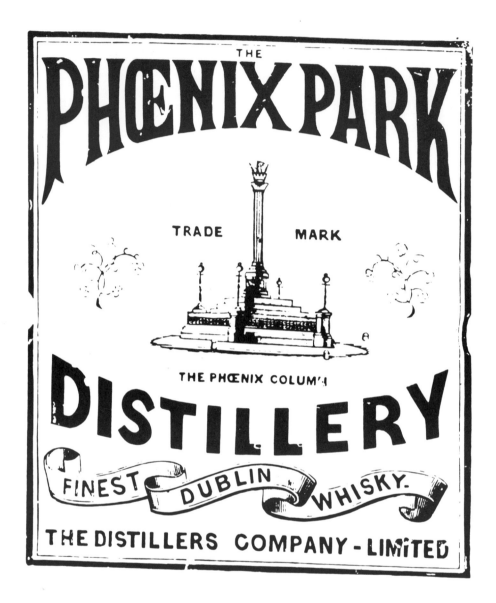

Ltd. of Edinburgh, their first such investment outside Scotland or England.

The distillery was set up in 1878 in what was a former spinning mill, on the upper reaches of the Liffey, near the scenic Salmon Leap. It had four pot stills, six bonded warehouses and employed about 60 workers. It had no steam power, its heating and electric lighting motivation was generated by a giant water wheel reaching across the Liffey, 70 feet in breadth and 18 feet in diameter. It had an output of about 350,000 gallons, mostly exported to London and the British colonies. The distillery manager was John A. Haig.

An article in *The Irish Builder* of December 12, 1901, said the original building was constructed in 1856 as a flax spinning factory by William Dargan, the great contractor who built Ireland's first railway, the Dublin-Kingstown line (Westland Row-Dun Laoghaire, 1832-37). The building was converted into a distillery in 1878 at a cost of between £30,000 and £40,000.

In his book *Scotch Made Easy* (Hutchinson: 1959) Ross Wilson quotes from a prospectus issued on behalf of the proposed new distilling company:

"... It is a very important fact that the quality and reputation of Dublin-made whiskey is at present, in general, equivalent to a premium of one shilling per gallon, or an additional 25 percent over whiskey made in other parts of Ireland.

'The demand for Irish whiskey is practically unlimited at present. The deliveries of Scotch whiskey into Ireland (principally at Belfast for reshipment) and into England (which is sold to the consumer as Irish whiskey) it is calculated would equal the produce of twenty such distilleries as the proposed one.

"There are considerably over one hundred whiskey distilleries in Scotland, in Ireland not twenty, while the demand for Dublin whiskey is estimated at more than five-fold that for Scotch at present.

"It may be safely asserted that Irish whiskey, if sold at a fair price and of good quality, would in great measure displace its Scotch rival...

"Irish whiskey, there can be little doubt, will eventually, from its extreme purity and wholesome character as a stimulant, almost completely displace other stimulants such as brandy, rum and gin..."

The Phoenix Park Distillery, however, had a comparatively short life span. It ceased production in 1921, an unsettled period in Ireland, both politically and commercially.

Cork Distilleries Co. Ltd.

What was probably the first major amalgamation of distilleries in these islands took place in 1867 when the Cork Distilleries Company Ltd. was formed by the merger of Midleton and four Cork city distilleries, North Mall, the Green, Watercourse and John Street.

Old Midleton completed 150 years of distilling history in 1975, when it dutifully surrendered to the magnificent new Irish Distillers complex which will carry on the name and tradition for perhaps another 150 years.

The original building dates from the year 1796 and was designed as a woollen mill by Marcus Lynch who leased the lands from Viscount Midleton. A few years later Lynch sold the property to the Government who turned it into a military barracks during the Napoleonic wars. In 1823 the Government sold the building to the Archbishop of Cashel, the Viscount's brother, for just £1,750. The Archbishop died the following year and the property reverted to Lord Midleton. He in turn disposed of the premises to James Murphy and his two brothers for £4,000.

The Murphys converted the building into a distillery, thus establishing the great Cork tradition with the industry, which has flourished through several generations and is now on the threshold of a new era of distilling. James Murphy was the man who consolidated the industry in the Cork region by carrying through the Cork Distilleries Company amalgamation in 1867 and became its first managing director. The Murphy family is still represented on the board of Irish Distillers Group today.

The Murphy brothers installed the world's largest pot still, 31,648 gallon capacity, in their distillery, which employed two hundred men. The huge still remained in use until 1975. There were two other pot stills and a patent or continuous still. Another full time survivor was an historic water wheel which continued to supply useful motive power.

Yours Ever Sincerely P. J. O'Flaherty

Left — P. J. (Paddy) O'Flaherty who gave his name to the famous 'Paddy Whiskey'.

Below — Old Distillery at Wise's Quay, Cork. Wise's Quay is named after Thomas Wise who had a distillery here, he became one of the wealthiest men in Cork. The old stone buildings are part of Irish Distillers depot, so to some degree the tradition continues.

The distinctive Midleton products included the renowned Paddy whisky, Hewitt's blended whiskey, Cork Dry Gin and Ireland's first vodka, Nordoff. Paddy, curiously, is the only Irish whiskey spelt in the Scotch manner, without the 'e.' There is an interesting story about how it got its name. In the 1920s Cork Distilleries had a very popular and resourceful company representative called Paddy O'Flaherty. The genial Paddy extolled the virtues of the company's fine old Cork whiskey so successfully among his trade customers that in submitting their repeat orders they simply asked for 'Paddy Flaherty's whiskey.' Astute company executives rewarded their diligent salesman by naming their product after him, a unique tribute in the whiskey trade.

The North Mall distillery was founded in 1779, built on the site of an old Dominican friary, the Abbey of St. Mary of the Island. Its first owners were Thomas and Francis Wise and it was inherited by Francis Wise junior who eventually sold to Cork Distilleries. Francis Wise died some years later leaving a reputed £3 million and large estates in Cork and Kerry.

The North Mall distillery ceased production in 1920 when fire destroyed a large portion of the premises. The old distillery covered an extensive area including spacious riverside grounds in which cottages were built for company employees. The administrative offices were located in Morrison's Island in the city centre, modern headquarters of Cork Distilleries Company, and included a showcase of trophies and medals awarded to the company at various international exhibitions for the excellence of its products, predominant among which was Wise's Old Pot Still whiskey.

In 1946 new buildings were erected in the grounds and modern equipment installed including an automatic bottling plant and vatting facilities. North Mall is now the main bottling and distribution centre for the southern region of Irish Distillers Group Ltd.

The Watercourse distillery dates back to 1793 and is chiefly associated with the Hewitt family who were represented from its earliest days until its acquisition by Cork Distilleries Company in 1867. The plant was utilised as a malting and stores during the 1880s and production transferred to North Mall, but the Hewitt distillery was reactivated towards the end of World War I and new machinery installed. Production, mostly potable grain spirit and industrial spirit, continued until 1975 when New Midleton came on stream.

The Green Distillery, in Thomas Davis Street, was founded in 1796. Its last private owner before the merger was George Waters. Daly's, of John Street, was started in 1807 and was closed after its incorporation with C.D.C. Some of the property was bought by J. J. Murphy and Company Ltd., of Lady's Well Brewery, Cork.

Belfast Distilleries

Belfast's two big distilleries closed down within a few years of each other in unfortunate circumstances causing serious industrial upset in the city and the loss of hundreds of well-paid jobs.

The Royal Irish Distilleries company was established in 1870 by William Dunville, whose family had been in the wine and spirit trade for many years. The distillery was built in the Grosvenor Road area of West Belfast. Barnard records that it was conceived and operated on an impressive scale. The company became the largest holders of pot still whiskey stocks in Ireland. A Coffey patent still was installed and by 1890 output exceeded two million gallons per year. Robert J. Dunville, who succeeded his uncle, guided the firm's progress with a sure hand. The company acquired the old-established Bladnoch distillery in Scotland and storage premises were opened in London, Liverpool and Glasgow.

Robert Dunville died in 1910 and the last member of the family to head the firm was his grandson who died unexpectedly in 1931. The effects of the industrial depression of the thirties were being felt by the firm and production was cut back. The Bladnoch distillery was sold at a loss and efforts were made to sell the Belfast plant without success. The company, which employed 400 workers, went into voluntary liquidation in late 1936.

Dunville's whiskey, as it was called, was a product of high quality and popularity at home and abroad. The decline and ultimate disappearance of this great firm was a tragic occurrence. A Belfast public park, near the site of the splendid distillery and donated by the company, commemorates the Dunville name.

The other main Belfast distillery of the time, owned by the Irish Distillery Company, was built at Connswater in 1886. When Barnard arrived there in the course of his spiritual wanderings the builders were still completing their work. He found a handsome red brick edifice of extensive proportions equipped with every new technical advance in the industry. The directors of the new company were all engaged in the whiskey business. There were two Coffey stills capable of distilling 4,000 gallons of wash per hour as well as pot stills. A smaller, older distillery, the Avoniel, with two Coffey stills, owned by William Higgins, was located in the same area. Both distilleries were eventually incorporated with David Watt and Company, owners of two distilleries in Derry, to form the extensive United Distillers Company Limited, registered in 1902.

Derry Distilleries

The Abbey Street distillery in Derry was said to be the biggest in the country. The malting house was over 300 feet long and nearly as wide. The buildings alone covered about eight acres with five huge warehouses and immense grain stores. It also had the largest steam engine in Ireland, 230 horse power. The plant had a yearly output of 1,260,000 proof gallons of grain whiskey by the end of the 19th century. The distillery came under the ownership of the Watt family, local merchants, about 1826. Andrew Alexander Watt also acquired the Waterside distillery in Derry around the same period. This was a smaller undertaking, manufacturing pot still whiskey. The United Distilleries Company, comprising the Belfast and Derry distilleries, became a formidable grouping in the international whiskey trade, but, like the Dunville distillery, it ran into economic difficulties and ultimate extinction.

E. B. McGuire in his book, *Irish Whiskey*, (Gill and Macmillan), a scholarly history of the distilling industry in Ireland, gives us an interesting account of the company's expansion and ultimate demise.

The company was exporting large quantities of grain spirit to various British companies for blending and rectifying. They also proposed extending their activities to Scotland by buying a defunct brewery in Edinburgh and converting it into a distillery. These moves caused some concern in the big Distillers Company conglomerate in Scotland who became worried about the danger of over-production and its possible serious repercussion on the market. The two groups came together to discuss production limits and eventually agreed on closer co-operation and exchange of shares. The Scottish company was to receive half the shares of U.D.C. who in turn would get a similar amount in value from D.C.L.

The Irish company later became involved in a new organisation called the Distillers Finance Corporation, embracing several blending and rectifying companies, with an exchange of respective share holdings. Moving further afield, United Distilleries went into the yeast manufacturing business, and joined with an American yeast firm, Fleischmann and Company, to set up a new firm called the International Yeast Company.

These unilateral financial manoeuvrings by the Irish company were not looked upon with any favour by the Distillers Company, especially as the new yeast company would be in direct competition with their own United Yeast Company. Consequently, when the Distillers Financial Corporation encountered trading difficulties, the Distillers Company succeeded in taking it over. With the additional U.D.C. shares involved in the purchase deal, the Scottish combine had now acquired a controlling interest in the Irish group. The Belfast and Derry distilleries continued to operate for some years but eventually, in the middle 1920s, their trading activities gradually came to an end.

Coleraine Distillery

The old-established distillery in Coleraine, Co. Derry, has been part of the Bushmills organisation since the 1930s. The distillery, about eight miles from the Bushmills location, was established in 1820. In the 1880s it was taken over by Robert A. Taylor who had extensive business interests in the area. Barnard was immensely impressed by the Coleraine distillery which, he said, was among the best he had ever seen for cleanliness, order and regularity. "The stillmen delighted in their work," he wrote. "They regarded the old pot stills with

veneration. They kept them shining like gold and every bit of brasswork was as polished and bright as for a jeweller's showcase."

The Coleraine product of the time was a 10 year-old pure malt whiskey and had a very high reputation. It was supplied to the House of Commons in London for many years. The distillery remained under the Taylor family name until its incorporation with Bushmills.

Comber Distillery

The village of Comber, about eight miles from Belfast, once boasted two distilleries, known as the Upper and the Lower, under the one ownership. The upper distillery, much the larger, was a former brewery, purchased and converted about 1825 by John Millar, who two years later acquired the smaller distillery.

The ownership changed over the years and the smaller distillery was closed. The Comber pot still whiskey enjoyed a fine reputation for more than a century and survived the two world wars. It remained a small independent firm with limited resources but, eventually, changing trends and trading difficulties brought about its closure in 1953.

Tullamore Distillery

One of the most inspired slogans ever applied to a brand of whiskey, 'Give every man his Dew,' certainly made Tullamore Dew universally known. The 'Dew' artfully incorporates the initials of the company, D. E. Williams Ltd.

The Tullamore distillery was founded in 1829 by Michael Molloy and in 1857 the property passed into the hands of his nephew, Bernard Daly. Thirty years later Daly's son, Captain Bernard Daly, succeeded to the ownership. Much of the captain's time was taken up by equestrian pursuits—international polo, hunting and breeding thoroughbred horses. In order to allow himself sufficient time to follow his sporting interests, Capt. Daly appointed a new general manager of the distillery. It was a move which brought remarkable developments in the company's fortunes.

Daniel E. Williams was given his first job in the distillery as a boy of fifteen and made his way up to the post of engineer. Capt. Daly was so impressed by the man's exceptional abilities and diligence that he placed him in complete charge. Under Williams's dynamism the distillery assumed new dimensions. Business expanded rapidly with additional home and overseas markets. The premises were enlarged and new equipment installed. Daniel Williams remained with the firm for almost sixty years, a charitable man, held in high esteem by workers and associates. He died in 1921 and was succeeded by his son, Captain John Williams.

In 1903 the distillery was formed into a private company, B. Daly & Co. Ltd., with the shares held by Capt. Daly and the Williams family. In 1931 Capt. Daly resigned from the board and the Williams family acquired his shares. The distillery was closed down in 1954 but the Tullamore district is still associated with several Williams business enterprises, notably the Irish Mist Liqueur Co. Ltd.

Irish Mist, Ireland's first liqueur, has a legendary background which reaches down through the centuries to a traditional Irish beverage known as heather wine, a cordial made from whiskey and heather honey to a secret recipe. The formula was lost with the defeat of the proud Irish armies by the Elizabethan and Williamite forces in the 16th and 17th centuries, which led to the great exodus of Irish fighting men (the Wild Geese) to the continent of Europe, known as the Flight of the Earls.

It was Daniel E. Williams who revived interest in the ancient recipe, which he felt must have been preserved through the generations. The Williams company were experimenting in this direction when, in 1948, an Austrian refugee arrived in Tullamore and produced a recipe for a liqueur which he said had been with his family for generations, but was of Irish origin. After careful trials the Williams family were convinced that here indeed was the long-lost secret of the legendary heather wine. They called it Irish Mist and today the liqueur is sipped and relished in many countries of the world.

Kilbeggan Distillery

The Kilbeggan distillery in Co. Westmeath, formerly

The Virtues of Age

DIRECT FROM A 200 YEAR OLD DISTILLERY

Locke's
LIQUEUR
IRISH WHISKEY

known as the Brusna distillery and later as Locke's, is reputed to go back to the year 1757. When John Locke took over the business in the 1840s he extended the plant considerably, and his two sons who succeeded him, John Edward and James H. Locke, carried out futher expansions. Four pot stills, built by Millar of Dublin, were in use, and an annual output exceeding 150,000 gallons was achieved. About seventy men were employed and Barnard tells us that the aged and infirm were always pensioned off or assisted. The firm was converted into a limited company in 1893 and prospered until the late 1920s when the post-war depression era badly affected the whiskey trade and put many distilleries out of business.

In 1947 the directors of Locke's distillery decided to offer it for sale as a going concern. This move gave rise to a set of circumstances that made rather sensational newspaper headlines and centred around the activities of a three-man syndicate of aliens, reportedly interested in taking over the distillery.

Strong allegations were made in the Dáil about the political patronage affecting government Departments and reported attempts by the syndicate to get 60,000 gallons of whiskey for sale on the 'black market' in England. Following a resolution passed by the Dáil Éireann on November 6th, 1947, the Taoiseach, Éamon de Valera, ordered a judicial public inquiry to be set up, under a tribunal of High Court judges, to investigate and report on the allegations. After an exhaustive and detailed examination of the evidence and statements the tribunal found that there was no foundation for the allegations.

Two members of the syndicate had earlier been ordered to leave Ireland following police inquiries into their backgrounds. One of the men, placed on the Dun Laoghaire to Holyhead ferry under police escort, disappeared without trace during the journey. He had carried a British passport, obtained, it was stated, under false pretences, and was allegedly sought by the police in England in connection with criminal charges.

After the storm has settled the now famous distillery continued in business for some years but in 1953 it was compelled by the economic recession to close down.

Galway Distillery

The only licensed distillery of any prominence in Galway or the province of Connacht was Persse's, located at Nun's Island on the Corrib river which supplied its motive power. The product, labelled Persse's Galway Whiskey, attained an annual output of 400,000 gallons by 1890.

Originally the distillery was owned by the Joyce family and was bought by Thomas Persse in 1840. Earlier the building had been converted into a woollen mill and enjoyed some prosperity for a period but it was restored to its original purpose by the new owner. Henry Persse, who succeeded his father in the early 1880s, built up a thriving business which continued until about 1915 when wartime difficulties forced it to close down.

Limerick Distillery

The Thomond Gate distillery in Limerick, owned by Archibald Walker, a Scotsman who also had distilling interests in Glasgow and Liverpool, dated from the early 19th century. When Barnard arrived there in 1887 he likened its appearance to an old baronial castle; it had two small inner courtyards and was reached by a stone archway. A high railed platform built over the huge water tanks gave splendid views of the Shannon, Limerick city and, in the far distance, counties Clare and Tipperary.

The well-equipped still house, a model of its kind, according to Barnard, had three copper pot stills, one of them the newest of its type, built by Millar's of Dublin. There were four large bonded stores, seventy five men were employed and output reached 300,000 gallons a year, most of it for export.

Barnard visited the residence of the manager in the distillery grounds and formerly occupied by the owner. He described it as a fine mansion of great antiquity, situated on the banks of the Shannon "and commanding views that could not be surpassed by any other house in Ireland." From the bay window of one of the drawing rooms one could look down on the sailing and fishing boats passing just below.

Monasterevan Distillery

One of the many small family-owned distilleries that enjoyed a good local trade was the Monasterevan distillery, in Co. Kildare, built by John Cassidy in 1784. It remaining with the family until its closure in 1921 after 137 years in business.

Like most other Irish distilleries of its type, Monasterevan was efficiently run and well equipped. It had a pleasantly rural atmosphere and twice weekly during the grain-buying season the place would be thronged with farmers in their carts. The corn buyer's office had a stone-paved floor and here the farmers would arrive with their stocks of barley. These would be examined and, if purchased, parcelled and numbered, and the price registered.

The distillery comprised five solid stone buildings. It had a mash house built in the shape of a beehive. During the construction of the conical roof, it is said, some of the workmen left the job, fearing that it would fall on them before the keystone was placed. Two drying kilns had floors of perforated tiles with furnaces below. Small boys were employed periodically to prick the clogged holes in the tiles in order to maintain proper ventilation. Top production reached about 200,000 proof gallons a year, most of which was sold locally or to other distilleries for mixing and blending.

Just a year or so after being built the distillery was set on fire and badly damaged; subsequently it was reconstructed and extended. The arson, it appears, was perpetrated by an ex-employee in a fit of rage after he had been dismissed. This incident is related in an article in the Kildare Archaeological Society Journal, Vo. XI, No. 4, 1969, by John Holmes, whose father purchased the former distillery in 1934 to house his engineering business.

Dundalk Distillery

The Dundalk distillery owned by Malcolm Brown & Co., and known as the Patent and Old Still Distillers, was one of the most extensive in Ireland outside the cities. In the late 19th century its annual output was in the region of 800,000 proof gallons, both grain and pot still, with more than 100 employees. Five stills were utilised, including a Coffey patent still. There were nine bonded stores containing over 7,000 cases of whiskey. The transport fleet consisted of seven horse-drawn carts which conveyed the produce to nearby boat and rail terminals. There was also a well-drilled and equipped fire brigade, with 26 firemen.

Alfred Barnard tells us that the original site of the buildings was developed by Dutch settlers who engaged in cambric manufacturing. He was greatly impressed by the engine room, which, he noted, housed a wonderful machine of 40 horse power, then fifty years old, and a powerful donkey engine, feeding five boilers each 20 feet long and 16 feet diameter.

The distilling building was taken over by Malcolm Brown in 1800 and continued in family ownership until economic decline inevitably overtook the Dundalk company and the distillery was put up for sale about 1912. It was bought by the Distillers Company of Scotland for a reputed £160,000. They carried on the business until 1926 when the distillery was finally closed.

Drogheda Distillery

The nearby town of Drogheda also had a notable distilling tradition in the 19th century, with several small distilleries. The largest, and last, of these was owned by John Woolsey who had extensive brewing interests in neighbouring Castlebellingham. Distilling in Drogheda ceased before the end of the century and the buildings were acquired by the noted ale brewing firm of Cairnes about 1930. This company was eventually taken over by the Guinness organisation.

Bandon Distillery

The Bandon, Co. Cork, distillery owned by Richard L. Allman and James C. Allman, was one of the more notable of the provincial distilleries. It employed more men than any other distillery outside the main cities and produced more than 200,000 proof gallons a year of pot still as well as pure malt whiskey.

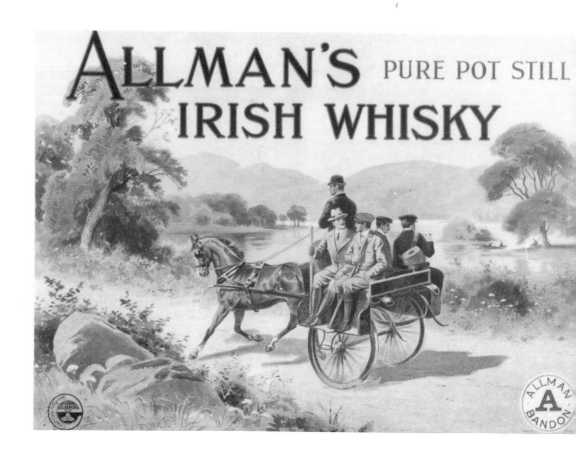

The original main building was said to be a manorial mill dating back to 1700 and was converted to a distillery in 1826 by the Allman family. The main malt house was reputed to be the largest in Britain or Ireland with the exception of that in the Guinness brewery in Dublin.

When Alfred Barnard visited the Bandon distillery in 1886 he described it as resembling a village of industries with skilled coppersmiths, carpenters, engineers, fitters, painters and harness makers all busily and happily engaged. The distilling plant was expertly maintained and efficiently run.

When Barnard arrived there he said the scene resembled a market fair day. Farmers' sons in their Sunday best were bringing in their home-grown corn. About seventy horse-carts loaded with barley were lined up awaiting their turn to deliver to the granaries. A staff of clerks weighed and tested the corn and dispatched the bundles by patent lifts to the grinding or malting floors. The distillery took in about 1,200 barrels of corn every day from early October until Christmas and paid out about £800 a day to the farmers. The Bandon distillery had a large trade with Britain and the British colonies. Unusually, the company bottled its own whiskey for export. The Bandon distillery ceased production in the mid-1920s.

Wexford Distillery

The Bishopswater distillery, in Wexford town, was built in 1827 by a group of local businessmen. It was made of solid Wexford stone and built on the slope of a hill. The principal director was Nicholas Devereux, a member of a prominent Wexford family, who eventually acquired control. The annual production, which reached about 100,000 proof gallons of pot still, served a mainly local market, although it enjoyed a useful trade with English and Scottish wholesale merchants and blenders. The distillery continued in production until the early 1920s.

Birr Distillery

A distillery at Birr, Co. Offaly, owned by R. and J. Walker, was established in 1805. A striking limestone

NICHOLAS DEVEREUX & Cº.
Distillers.

Bishops Water Distillery, WEXFORD.
Established 1827.

building, it was approached by a long avenue winding from the river bank up to an ivy-draped stone archway giving access to the main building. The distillery employed about forty workers and produced 200,000 gallons a year of pot still whiskey. It enjoyed prosperity for many years with a strong local sale and a fair export trade with England but it eventually closed down during the late 1890s.

Kilkenny Distillery

Kilkenny had its Mount Warrington Distillery. An advertisement in the Kilkenny *Moderator* in the year 1836 and quoted in the *Old Kilkenny Review*, November 6, 1953, offered the premises for sale or rent. The distillery was located on the River Nore and close to Kilkenny city.

Kilkenny is perhaps more associated with the brewing industry, notably the famous Smithwicks brewery which is built on the site of the ancient St. Francis Abbey. It is thought likely that beer was brewed in the Franciscan friary as early as the 14th century. Excavation and restoration work has been carried out on the site in recent years.

The Maltings on the Lee at Cork, a good example of how a beautiful disused industrial building has found a new use as part of University College, Cork.

Chapter 19

What the Experts Say

 "WHISKEY IS essentially an Irish question. The mellowness, the generosity and the wholesomeness of that Irish specialty...Irish whiskey owes its incomparable flavour to the more delicate and ethereal essences evolved from the best grain procurable by the distiller skilled in the management of the pot still. Its purity, wholesomeness and suitability have enabled it not alone to hold its own, but to a constantly growing extent surpass most other stimulants."

—George Agustus Sala (1829-95)

"A pure well-matured product of mild character, rich in fragrant ethers."

—Sir Charles Cameron

"A sovereign drink—the chroniclers declare
If it be taken orderlie—beware
Of surfeit. Sip it and you'll find
It sloweth age and brighteneth the mind.
It keepeth head from whirling, teeth from chattering,
Tongue from lisping and throte from rattling,
It keepeth heart from swelling, guts from rumbling,
The hands from shivering and the bones from
    crumbling."

—Theoricus

"Usquebaugh...is a compounded distilled spirit being drawn on aromaticks, and the Irish sort is particularly distinguished for its pleasant and mild flavour."

—Dr. Samuel Johnson

140

"Never was philtre found with such power
To charm and bewilder as this we are quaffing.
The magic began when in Autumn's rich hour
As a harvest of gold in the field it stood laughing.
There having by nature's enchantment been filled
With the balm and the boon of the kindliest weather,
The wonderful juice from its core was distilled
To enliven such hearts as we have here brought
    together."
                                    —*Thomas Moore*

"Malachi Horan's recipe for a long and contented
life—Plenty of whiskey, and the hard work necessary to
get the money to buy it."
                                    —*Malachi Horan*

"Dr. W. G. Grace, the famous cricketer, always drank a
double Irish whiskey and soda, plus a dash of angustura
bitters, on every match day, both at lunch and at the
close of play—and W.G. was still hitting centuries at the
grand old cricketing age of 55."
                                    —*Wine Mine*

"The light music of whiskey falling into a glass—an
agreeable interlude."
                                    —*James Joyce*

"As a substance for ships to sail on, water is unsur-
passed."
                                    —*James Stephens*

"There is no such thing as a large whiskey."
                                    —*Oliver St. John Gogarty*

'If an angel out of Heaven
Gives you something else to drink,
Thank her for her kind intention
And pour it down the sink."
                                    —*G.K. Chesterton*

"Ireland is a country where, except for a species of moonshine called potheen, there isn't any bad liquor. The
general level strikes me as positively Himalayan."
                                    —*The Esquire Drink Book*

"Irish whiskey is part of Ireland's heritage, as are its fine linens, Waterford glass or tweeds. It is the distilled essence of the country, a product of the earth—of clean pure water from fathomless underground springs and brisk tumbling rivers, and golden barley from Irish farmlands. Its production involves thousands of people. A thriving distilled spirits industry means an industry exporting Irish whiskey to world markets."

—*Milton Greenberg*
Managing Editor, Associated
Beverage Publications, New York, 1978

'Health and long life to you,
Land without rent to you,
A child every year to you,
And may you die in Ireland."

—*Old Irish toast*

IRISH COFFEE

Cream — rich as an Irish brogue
Coffee — strong as a friendly hand
Sugar — sweet as the tongue of a rogue
Whiskey — smooth as the wit of the land.

Heat a steamed whiskey goblet. Pour in a jigger of Irish whiskey, add three cubes of sugar. Fill goblet with strong, black HOT coffee. Stir well, and top off with rich cream poured over a spoon, or with cream slightly whipped.

Index